**about
understanding**

about
understanding
—ideas and observations
on cross-cultural
communication

by
andreas
fuglesang

dag hammarskjöld foundation 1982

The Dag Hammarskjöld Foundation was established in 1962 in memory of the late Secretary-General of the United Nations. The opinions expressed in its publications are those of the authors and do not necessarily reflect the views of the Foundation.

General editor: Sven Hamrell

The Dag Hammarskjöld seminars on communication in the fields of nutrition, child health care, and appropriate technology in Third World countries and the follow-up work, including the publication of this book, were financed by grants from the Swedish International Development Authority.

Dag Hammarskjöld Foundation
Övre Slottsgatan 2
752 20 Uppsala, Sweden

ISBN 91-85214-09-4
Printed in Sweden by Motala Grafiska, Motala

To my son Kim

He who knows much
speaks with silence
Amharic proverb

contents

preface

The 1975 Dag Hammarskjöld Report (*What Now: Another Development*) devoted one of its ten main points to the need for improving public information and cross-cultural understanding:

Citizens have a right to inform and be informed about the facts of development, its inherent conflicts and the changes it will bring about, locally and internationally.

Under present conditions, information and education are only too often monopolized by the power structure, which manipulates public opinion to its own ends.

A global effort should be made to give the new international relations their human dimension and to promote the establishment of genuine cooperation between peoples on the basis of equality and recognition of their cultural, political, social and economic diversity. The image of the Other should reach each of us, stripped of the prevailing ethnocentric prejudices, which are the characteristic feature of most of the messages currently transmitted.

Such an effort should be concerned both with information and with education in the broadest sense of the word; it should be directed towards 'conscientization' of citizens to ensure their full participation in the decision-making process.

Since this was written, an ever growing importance has been attached to the communications *problématique* as is evident from the debates in UNESCO and in the General Assembly of the United Nations as well as from the work undertaken by the International Commission for the Study of Communication Problems (the MacBride Commission), whose main results were published in 1979 under the title *Communication and Society Today and Tomorrow: Many Voices, One World.* But while most of these efforts to transform the present international information structures and to redress existing imbalances have been made in a fairly abstract manner and at a rather high political level, there have also been a number of attempts to tackle the problems of communication at the grassroots level. An important contribution of the latter type has been made over the last ten years by Andreas Fuglesang, who in 1972 organized the first Dag Hammarskjöld seminar on applied communication in the Third World and who has since then directed or actively participated in three more Dag

9

Hammarskjöld seminars, resulting in four publications carrying his name and testifying to the conceptual and practical value of his work.

As Andreas Fuglesang is well aware, we are now entering the 'information age', characterized by an ever increasing rate of innovation, which sees computers, computerized automatons and processing systems outdated almost as soon as they leave the assembly plants. While it cannot be denied that new and astonishingly successful applications of this electronic technology are made almost every day, it will take some time before it is possible to assess the impact of the 'information revolution' on the Third World and on South-North relations. But what may be said with some certainty is that we now, in the industrialized countries, are witnessing a widening gap between the quantity of information being disseminated and the quality of communication taking place between individuals and that the explosive developments in media technology have done little to prevent cultural isolation and alienation. A mere 100 years ago, words were largely spoken or written between human beings. Now, words are spoken to and from machines. It is somewhat disconcerting to contemplate what will happen when the Third World is hit by the full implications of this development.

But however menacing these new technological developments may be or whatever hopes they may hold for the future, there still prevails in many villages and urban communities in Scandinavia—as in many other parts of the world—an old political belief that one can achieve understanding and solidarity among human beings. Understanding in an international context is likely to be achieved when the people in such local communities perceive that the problems of communities in other countries and cultures are inextricably linked to their own. When this perception takes root, the 'sacrifices' necessary for the transition to Another Development are more likely to be made. The ultimate task of development communication is therefore to expand these areas of local community solidarity until a dimension is achieved which promotes a continuing global dialogue between the cultures of the world.

Andreas Fuglesang's new book should be read and judged in this context. The Dag Hammarskjöld Foundation initiated this work by requesting an updated version of Fuglesang's popular book *Applied Communication in Developing Countries: Ideas and Observations*, originally published in 1973. Fortunately, instead of an update, a new book 'about understanding' emerged. Thanks to Fuglesang's extensive Third World experience, the book has not become an abstract discourse but retains its practical orientation. Fuglesang introduces new and bold perspectives in his analysis of the role of communications in social and economic development. His argument that social transformation can be described in terms of social information processing provides new and valuable insights. But as a practical guide to the issues of development communication, the book is primarily focussed on the dilemmas confronting the development workers in the Third World. In this book, they will be gratified to find many valuable observations and ideas that they can apply to their respective work situations.

With his unfailing trust in people, his advocacy of people's ability to decide the direction of their development, and his demonstration of solutions found by people, Fuglesang has made a significant contribution to the conception of Another Development and to the discussion of the approaches and strategies involved in reaching this goal.

One of Andreas Fuglesang's central contentions is that cross-cultural communication must concern itself with the fundamental question of language. Under the overwhelming onslaught of the media technology, the role played by language in cross-cultural communication has been given only secondary importance. The failure of the ideals of international understanding and solidarity may, however, be accounted for in part by the fact that we have not built into our practical approach a component for an emphathetic appreciation of what our sisters and brothers in other cultures really have to say. It is this challenging objective that Andreas Fuglesang has set for himself in this new book *About Understanding*, which is likely to have a profound impact on the development and direction of the emerging field of cross-cultural communication.

> *Sven Hamrell*
> Executive Director
> Dag Hammarskjöld Foundation

Uppsala, January 1982.

introduction

Writing a book on cross-cultural communication is like walking in the dark on a stony path. The problem is more one of seeing than one of writing. Ludwig Wittgenstein says it simply: Don't think—look! With that he makes it clear that understanding is more a state of mind than a mental process. Understanding is the state of seeing. Unfortunately for the writer —and the reader—understanding is not the process of writing about the seeing.

One practical problem in cross-cultural communication is that a writer from one culture is safe when he looks at another culture, but the moment he starts writing about it, he is in trouble. It is my belief that a culture cannot be justly described in the concepts of another culture. It can truly be rendered only through its own means of expression.

Social anthropologists, social psychologists and sociologists work hard at making their disciplines into sciences. However, their academic history is convincing evidence that we all perceive the world through the contemporary prejudice. In this, the writer is no exception. Yet it is from these disciplines that, rightly, we should expect guidance.

International understanding is more precarious than ever and solidarity is at its lowest ebb. This demise exists at a time when we should be able to see that cultural differences are superficial phenomena. In my experience, it is the similarities in man's many endeavours to control his reality—not the differences—that are impressive culturally. Each of us needs to act to rectify the social, economic and attitudinal disparities and prejudices which permeate the world. Posterity can muse upon whether our progress was made by science or by seeing.

I am grateful to photographers E. Dahlschen and B.E. Gyberg who have contributed substantially to the photography in this book. Special thanks goes to social anthropologist D. Chandler, for the valuable advice and criticism of the content and, not least, for the skilled editing of my shaky English. M. Max-Neef deserves thanks for many useful comments on the script. But most of all I am indebted to Mukahamubwatu, Lute Mirla, Godson Handoma, Kassaye Negash, Acmajid Asha and all the other farmers and housewives I have met in Africa and elsewhere who made the venture of this book worthwhile.

Geneva/Nairobi
March 1980

Andreas Fuglesang

1
the arrogance of aristotle

Question: *All the cocks in Kasombe Village are white.*
Lute Mirla saw a cock in Kasombe Village.
What colour was the cock she saw?

Answers: *Lute Mirla went to the market yesterday to sell two chickens.*
Lute Mirla has a sister she goes to see in Kasombe Village.
Ask Lute Mirla when she comes back.

THE SYLLOGISM

The self-evidence and eternal truth of the syllogism are immaterial to the Bemba villagers in the Northern Province of Zambia. This is not due to a lack of ability to understand the syllogism, but because it has no relevance to the problems of survival in the sunburnt reality of Bembaland and because the language habitually used by the Bembas allows them to describe, interpret and understand reality in a different manner from an English speaker. Let us not conclude that this is a limitation. Rather it may be an expansion of human understanding which has been lost on the way. Speakers of a Bantu language have verbal instruments which they use to dissect nature. To be sure, they dissect nature in a different way from the speakers of European languages, but they do dissect it. As gracefully as the Greeks or not is hardly the issue.

THE NEGATION—THE LOGICAL UNIVERSE

Hodgeson Mwanza in Luwingu does not regard the *negation* and the *logical universe* very highly either, for example tree/not tree. This thing is a tree and everything else which is not this tree is the rest of the world. Either it is 'tree' or it is 'not tree'. It cannot be something in between or something else at the same time. It cannot be both a house and a tree.

Of course it can! Hodgeson Mwanza is tolerant with what he surely considers my mental confusion. He explains that the tree is the tree which

15

provides shade from its branches, which supplies firewood for his wife, and which is the abode of his ancestors. The tree *is* several things at the same time. For Hodgeson Mwanza, no logical contradiction exists. As an alien to Hodgeson's linguistic perceptions, my problem lies in the language I am habitually using as I endeavour to describe Hodgeson's thoughts about the tree. He does not experience 'the tree as the abode of his ancestors'—that is a distinction in my language. Rather he experiences 'the abode of his ancestors' at the same time as he experiences 'the tree'. This simultaneity of experiences is a reality of such force that the mere thought of cutting down the tree and invoking the wrath of these spirits is as shattering to him as the action itself. However, this does not hinder Hodgeson in applying another kind of logic when required.

ABSTRACT CLASSIFICATION

Bana Enifa, probably 29 years old, ten children born, four of them dead, weeds the endless rows of her maizefield with one more about to be born, one on her back and one weeping into her skirt. For her, what value is there in representing objects by a system of *abstract classification* instead of by their concrete functional or perceptual quality?

'Mama Enifa, what is this?'

'Paw paw!'

'And what is this?'

'Mango!'

'How is a paw paw like a mango?'

She does not answer they are both 'fruits'. She has no use for the 'class of fruits'. Bana Enifa answers: 'I can eat paw paw! I can eat mango!' She may also say, 'They are round.' To her, the important point is evidently what 'use' she can make of a thing or what she can 'see of likeness' between things here and now. People develop the language they need. It is important to note that adjectives such as 'round', 'square' or 'triangular' do not exist in Bemba. There is a term indicating 'circularity', which Bana Enifa applies to such objects as a pot, pan, frog, etc. Another term, indicating 'triangularity', she would use for such objects as an arrowhead, bow, etc.

A similar notion is found in Swahili. For example, *pembe tatu*, which means triangle, is literally 'horn-three'. *Pembe* means horn, elephant tusk, or various horn-like objects such as a powder-flask, an angle or a corner.

Lute Mirla, Hodgeson Mwanza, Bana Enifa, and all the others . . . The group under the village tree is mostly patient and polite in its answers and they suffer the bewilderment of the educator gracefully. When the group sometimes responds with silence, why does the educator interpret it as intransigence? A verbal formulation of everyday problems and work activities is not common in their language. Village people usually acquire their knowledge from handling things, not from reading books.

I have noticed that when Lute Mirla goes to see her sister, she stops for a while among the trees at the brink of the bush a good distance from the hut, calling out loudly, 'Hodi! Hodi!' Among the Bembas it is polite to notify those inside of one's arrival, thus avoiding embarrassment and giving them time to prepare for the visitor. I have also noticed that the agricultural extension worker does not always do that, but then of course he is educated and knows better!

EDUCATIONAL TYRANTS

The government aims in a tacit manner to control people's thoughts through national literacy via the educationist, with the elaborate ignorance of his Ph.D. thesis on pedagogical methods, via the primary school teacher with western learning modules, and via the agricultural extension worker or the adult literacy instructor preoccupied with finding a new job in the city. Through no fault of their own, these people develop into educational tyrants. They have been oppressed by an educational system which has taught them by attitude and implication that they shall meet poverty, ignorance and intransigence in the village—and that is the reason why they often meet precisely that.

THINKING TOOLS AND ARROGANCE

The *syllogism*, the *negation*, the *abstract classification* have become the attributes of intellectual skills and wisdom. While the law of contradiction in the syllogism or the law of the excluded middle in the negation may be useful thinking tools for some people in some life situations, they are not necessarily useful for all people in all situations. Science is only one of man's many attempts to control his reality. In some respects, this approach may be a more successful one. The Aristotelian heritage in western or European culture is embodied in our scientific attitude to reality, but being an attitude of fundamental desire to change reality, it carries with it a seemingly inseparable arrogance towards those who think otherwise. It may become clear to us one day that the triumph of European culture is also its fallacy. The speculatively sophisticated Greeks have their solid share in our past and our future, so do the rough Roman legions—and our Christian heritage? Man is created in God's image? What a disloyalty to the other creatures on this lonesome globe of ours to assume so.

DISRESPECT FOR OTHER CULTURES

The significant feature of European culture is not only its scentific and technological achievement. It also exudes disrespect for other cultures as well as insensitivity to the miraculous multiplicity of life and human behaviour.

Why are we so unable to understand that the people of each culture are cultured in their own way? There is no scientific evidence that civilization is synonymous with Aristotelian rationality. We are oblivious to the fact that all other cultures are described and interpreted in the concepts of our own culture. Our ethnocentrism is close to total. We are not able to sense how literally and daily we express our arrogance in our language. The negation is both a thought-tool and a thought-trap. Whilst *we* are the educated, other people are un-educated. Hodgeson Mwanza and Bana Enifa are *il*-literate, *ir*-rational, *pre*-logical and, let us add, *un*-productive and *in*-effective.

THE LANGUAGE-TRAP

Even the social anthropologists, despite their good intentions, are caught in the language-trap. In descriptions of what anthropologists have identified as the clan-system of a tribe, they have meted out their own measure of cultural bias. To analyse a tribal culture by distinguishing certain cultural elements is not exposing an ultimate cultural reality. By implication, it disintegrates the perception of the cultural whole. The clan element is simply a result arrived at through the process of analytic description itself. There is an answer in the way Hodgeson Mwanza expresses himself in his language. He does not perceive himself as 'a member of the leopard clan' or 'the crocodile clan'. He says, 'I am a leopard' or 'I am a crocodile.' He never uses the word 'clan'. He talks of *Bena Mbwili*, Leopard people, or *Bena Ng'wena*, Crocodile people.

When David Livingstone discovered 'The Thundering Waters', *Musi-o-Tunya*, he invented a different concept, 'The Victoria Falls'—but the reality of the Zambezi is undisturbed by the various names human beings might attach to it. It is important to perceive that the syllogism, the negation and the abstract classification are not discoveries of reality itself, of an eternal, absolute or self-evident truth—but simply linguistic inventions or conceptual tools which people find useful in varying degrees according to their life situation. With this realization, we may further understand that reality may be perceived in different ways depending on the language used to perceive it.

LINGUISTIC RELATIVITY

Cross-cultural communication is basically an attempt to attain agreement about subject matter among peoples of various cultures who speak different languages and who are unaware of the implications of their own respective speech habits. The notion of rationality or logical reasoning has in any culture the twist of that culture—so also in ours. When we indulge verbally in our logical faculties, we do not sense that the phenomenon of our language surrounds and controls us, the speakers, as an element outside our critical consciousness. The speaker of a language is like a swimmer moving effortlessly and at will in water while unaware that he is wet. Speakers of different languages are like swimmers in different ponds.

From this follows a principle of *linguistic relativity*, which has been explored by such thinkers as Ludwig Wittgenstein[1] and Benjamin Lee Whorf.[2] The principle holds that all observers are not led by the same physical evidence to the same picture of reality—unless their linguistic background is similar. Before cross-cultural communication can take place, the state of understanding itself must be better understood. Admittedly, this a challenging task, but it is the one attempted in this book.

2
the need for
demystifying our words

' *Why do you* Mzungu [*white person*] *not try to understand the minds of Africans more than their ability to work? You people do not understand your words do not belong to our minds.*'
Mukahamubwatu—old village woman,
Mapanza, Zambia

' . . . *A main source of our failure to understand is that we do not command a clear view of the use of our words.*'
Ludwig Wittgenstein

THE VIRTUE OF EXACTNESS

Our language is a technique of communication which we learn to master from our social environment. The words we learn have cultural connotations and reflect the prejudices, preferences, sympathies, aversions, superstitions, taboos or myths of that social environment. Mastering a language also means subjecting oneself to verbal habits and value judgements. We commit ourselves in casual, everyday use to meanings of words which, in more thoughtful moments, we may not want the words to have. For example, the word 'exact' has a connotation of something virtuous and, conversely, 'in-exact' has a connotation of something reproachable. From this arises the myth that the footnotes, references and verbal mannerisms of the academic are a more exact and therefore more valuable means of communication than the gutsy remarks of the man in the street or the proverbs of the elders under the village tree. We disregard the fact that these people and the academic do not necessarily have the same measurement of exactness. There is no single ideal of exactness.

DISTRUST IN PEOPLE

The myth sustains other strange illusions; for example, a judgement of reality made by a technical expert is more *trusted* than a judgement by a village farmer. We *disrespect* the ideas and opinions of people who happen to have their knowledge from sources other than books. Such misconceptions are also rampant in other connections. The notion that there is only one single correct way of talking and writing a language, that some dialects within a language are inferior, and that some languages have more sophisticated and expressive qualities than others are examples.

This leads to the idea that a foreign language represents colonial oppression or cultural domination or to the idea that a community will only safeguard its cultural identity by retaining its tribal language. The exponents of such ideas are all yielding to the same myth of paternalism, the general *distrust* in people's ability to cope with their lives. They are unaware that people develop the language they require; people learn a skill or acquire knowledge when they perceive it as a priority.

THE MYTH OF LOGICAL NECESSITY

A halo of superstitions and value judgements surrounds the concepts of *logic* and *logical necessity*. In the European culture, we consider more or less explicitly that it is desirable to be logical and, conversely, that it is undesirable to be illogical. To be very logical is even admirable! We attach universality to the concept of logical necessity and talk about 'the logical universe', 'the world of pure reason', 'a contradiction-free system', i.e. the negation, stone/not stone. In doing so, we overlook the simple circumstance that the universality is not a fact in reality, but only a feature in the linguistic picture we are using.

Necessity may be defined as a state where all alternatives except one are excluded—that is, excluded in the picture. The circumstance is really very simple and that is probably why we do not see it clearly! The only thing corresponding to a 'logical necessity' in our language is an arbitrary rule. The concept of 'logical necessity' in the Aristotelian syllogism or other logical mechanisms is simply a linguistic/social convention. Hence it is valid only for those who adhere to that convention. Consequently, to say a person from another culture has made an 'illogical statement' is really to express a racist attitude in the world of logic. That the language of formal logic is useful in some situations is another matter.

Ludwig Wittgenstein has illustrated so lucidly this conception of what 'logical necessity' is. We can only understand it by understanding the way we use our language.

THE MYTH OF TECHNOLOGY

Let us turn to other words which typically mystify and obscure our view of the way we use our language. *Technology* is one such word. A dominant myth emanates from the connotation that modern technology is for the good of mankind. It is desirable, clean, apolitical, efficient, in the long run cheap—and, above all, *technology is necessary*. Mass media and our modern social environment have propagandized the above connotations so effectively that they have become synonymous with the word 'technology'. In our sub-conscious, these connotations are the 'meaning of the word'. This is what we 'see' and by seeing this—perhaps because technology itself is so conspicuous—we overlook the fact that technology is a manifestation of a specific political system, namely a society based on capitalist principles, whether it is private or state capitalism is of minor importance in that connection. The shrewdness of the myth is demonstrated by the fact that we throw the blame for environmental pollution on the technology, whereas the real culprit is the political system. A world without modern technology is clearly thinkable and possible. We may even say with some justification that technology is not necessary.

THE MYTH OF DEVELOPMENT

Another myth in our language is projected through the word *development*. Intertwined with the myth of 'technology', it has many of the same connotations. In addition, its general use implies a value judgement, i.e. that good, desirable social development is synonymous with economic growth, a linear process of social change ending in the model of the modern western consumer society. The myth is that this is the only thinkable and possible direction of social development. The myth is also that the peoples of the Third World, in the serfdom of national debts, trade deficits and cultural oppression, have the freedom to define the direction of this development. This myth is sustained particularly by the North-South flow from the information monopolies.

The myth of development has devastating effects at the local human level. Use of such terms as un-developed and under-developed is outrageous. Those who have worked closely with people in the Third World cannot avoid seeing how it hurts to be called underdeveloped, to be told—explicitly or implicitly—that what you do is a mistake, that what you have done is inferior, and that you do not really know what you should do.

THERE IS NO PRIMITIVE MIND

Another mystification is represented in the word *primitive*. The word carries a disparaging implication and connotes a past stage in mankind's development or a stage from which society should progress. In general, it is used to indicate something of inferior quality: 'They live in a rather primitive house' or 'This institution has a primitive administration.' And then, of course, primitive is used as a characterization of Third World societies. The myth of 'the primitive mind' has been a particularly tenacious concept. It has been nurtured by 'the civilized citizen' since the days of Rome's battles with the barbarians and elevated by the romanticists since Rousseau. The myth of 'the primitive mind' gained momentum through the Freudian school of psychoanalysis and proliferates today in the much extolled educational psychology of J. Piaget.

It is essential to realize that the phenomenon of a primitive mind does not exist. This notion is a verbal tool of oppression deftly applied by the privileged under the cloak of scholarship. The thought processes of all people are functionally equivalent and can be inferred from people's linguistic behaviour.[3] There is no such thing as a stage of mental development which is 'lower' than that of an educated person. The notion that being 'illiterate' is something less desirable, less valuable than being literate derives from our misuse of language. People's thought processes are not different, but the classification systems they use to describe reality may be different.

This premise is fundamental to understanding and solving the problems of cross-cultural communication.

THE MYTH OF SOCIAL INSTITUTIONS

Let us take a closer look at the mythical connotations of social institutions such as the church, civil service, government, national defence forces, trade unions, industry, medical establishment, business community, finance, educational system, family and mass media. These institutions have specialized, complex functions, often incomprehensible and unexplained to the common man. Interlocked in an intricate interaction process, these institutions preserve and perpetuate the overall social system of which they are a part. This does not exclude the continuous power struggle between them. The common myth pervasively reinforced by the action of these institutions is that they are irreplaceable and irreproachable. Furthermore, they represent social respectability and common sense, law and order, the ethical standard, etc.

They have a history as long as settled man himself. They direct the process of social development through an agenda defined *for their actions*. Their pomp and power is awe-inspiring, but in the perspective of the universe, they are, indeed, little more than the faintly discernible patterns of interactions in an ant-hill.

CLUSTERS OF SOCIAL HABITS

We may command a clearer view of the words we use for social institutions by perceiving them simply as structured clusters of social habits. Institutions are social habits, i.e. systematic and perpetuated relationships and interactions between people.[4] We can also add that they are networks of vested interests with a potential for exploitation.

THE MYTHS OF THE EDUCATIONAL SYSTEM

In coping with the question of cross-cultural communication, we are dealing particularly with adult education, primary health care, nutrition, agriculture and similar issues. It is necessary, therefore, to devote more time to one of the social institutions of special significance, *the educational system*, often referred to as the formal and non-formal educational system. The concept of this institution requires demystifying and placing in alternative perspectives. The formal educational system is primarily concerned with instructing the next generation in the techniques and values of the dominant social system, thereby preserving and perpetuating a power structure. There is no reason to believe that the motivations and inventions of the educational system are of a nobler nature than those of other institutions. I am deeply suspicious of the professional attitudes and value judgements made by educators with particular reference to the educational system in the Third World. The educational élite is surviving its own ineptness by enlarging frenetically the bulwarks of its professed professionalism. Whose privilege is it to define the learning needs of the deprived and the poor? For too long, the educators have betrayed people with their professionalism. People are neither objects to be formed nor cases of ignorance to be treated. It is the thoughtfulness and creativity of the people which is the ultimate resource of any social development. It is not the privilege of the educator to list requirements in terms of knowledge and skills which are supposed to define an educated person. The educator behaves as if he were listing empirical facts when he is, in reality, uttering a series of value judgements.

In itself, it is an extremely dubious endeavour to assess people's learning needs from an outsider's perception of the social situation of others—and yet, educational programmes in health care, nutrition, family planning, etc. are continuously defined according to alien objectives and attitudes and launched in the villages. To formulate a definition of competence, the design of curricula and the development of course plans in this way is unrealistic, unviable and culturally oppressive. Extension workers and adult educators in the field are slow to realize that youngsters and adults alike may have priorities other than the educational priorities espoused by the educators. No learning experience will work unless the priorities of the people themselves are an integral part of a programme developed for their benefit.

There is a poisonous myth permeating our professional thinking. Our educators are taught—and teach—that ignorance is the cause of poverty. This sustains the deception that a structural change in society to eliminate the deeper causes is not necessary.

THE EDUCATED—A NEGATIVE CONTRIBUTION TO DEVELOPMENT?

Education has been promulgated as the key to modernization and development. Over the last two decades in Third World countries this has led to an enormous growth in allocations to educational systems. Many countries now set aside 20—25 per cent of the national budget for educational expenditures. The idea, conceived and maintained by the educationists, that a correlation exists between the stock of educated manpower and the rate of economic growth has not been borne out. It remains another myth. In fact, the evidence now seems to indicate that education, and in particular higher education, has reached a point in many Third World countries where it is making a negative contribution to their development.[5] The products of the educational system, the school leavers, are finding it difficult to secure employment. By and large, the unemployed are the educated and there are considerable differences in the rates of unemployment among labourforce groups with different levels of education—with particularly low unemployment rates among the illiterate urban population.[6] The Indian Educational Commission was already concerned with this problem in the early sixties, and stated: '. . . The educated élite thus become largely parasitical in character and the real productive workers are the unlettered peasants and artisans.'[7]

In view of this, we should perhaps agree that there are new dimensions to consider in the eulogy of education and the disrespect of the illiterate. A deeper understanding of the functions of educational institutions and the educational process itself is essential. By simplifying the concepts currently in vogue when describing this part of reality and by neutralizing the prevalent mythical terminology, a clearer view may be achieved.

SIMPLY, SOCIAL FORMATIONS

In the following pages, we shall look at social institutions and systems in their various configurations and with their various traditions as *social formations*. An insurance company is a specialized social formation. A village community is a social formation of a more general nature. A group of farmers who collaborate to build a storage house for their grain or who simply meet to discuss new methods is a social formation, although it may be of short duration or weak cohesion. The Catholic Church is a social formation of long duration and strong cohesion.

As previously indicated, social formations can be considered patterned ways of behaviour, clusters of social habits which are structured in various ways and for various purposes and which exhibit various degrees of duration and cohesion. This simple definition may lead to more fruitful thinking.

All too often, we ask the wrong questions. It serves no purpose to ask: What is a social formation? Rather, we should look at its function. What is the purpose of a social formation such as a women's club, a stock exchange, a university, a Freemason lodge, a group of tribesmen chasing a boar? All these formations have very specialized agendas for their activities and their members act in accordance with specialized codes of behaviour. What are the common features which allow us to classify them as social formations?

PROCESSING OF INFORMATION

One answer to the question may be that social formations *process information*. The attempt to qualify this view for our understanding of different social realities and the issue of cross-cultural communication will occupy the rest of this book.

It is reasonably clear that information processing is a common characteristic of social formations such as the British Broadcasting Corporation, Harvard University or the Adult Literacy Class in Mutondo Village. It is less clear, perhaps, in formations which have a conspicuous agenda or physical output such as the armed forces, an automobile manufacturing plant or a farmers' cooperative, which purchases fertilizer and seeds and organizes the storage and sale of the maize crop.

In what sense do such formations process information? A closer look reveals that they are, indeed, involved in a whole spectrum of information activities. They collect information; they record and store information; they have various systems for retrieving and presenting information; they transmit information to other social formations.

For the farmers' cooperative, information processing ranges from collection of data on fertilizer prices and distribution of the data to members to records of membership fees, quantities of maize delivered by each member, and distribution of the yearly accounts and report to members.

SOCIAL FORMATIONS—AND TRANSFORMATIONS

As mentioned, social formations vary in duration. A hunting party of tribesmen is transient; once the hunt is over, the group changes form. Institutions such as the church or the government, however, convey a feeling of longevity and permanence. This derives from the time perspective of the observation. In the time perspective of the universe there are no social formations, there are only *social transformations*. This concept carries a very specific definition. To transform means 'to make change in form' and *transformation* means 'a change in form'. Such a 'new' change in the form of a social formation is no more permanent than the 'old' form. Transformation, therefore, really comes to mean 'the process of change', the continuous change of form which takes place.

It is important to note that the concept of the transformation is concerned with *what* happens, not with *why* it happens.[8] *Panta rei*, everything is in flux. When we say that change occurs continuously, we encounter problems with our language. No words are available to describe what happens inside a continuum except the notion of 'the infinite step'. This is cumbersome and, for some of us, mentally unhealthy. We shall, therefore, think of social transformation as happening in finite steps. Although we know there is a continuum of social transformation, we choose to say that at any definite point in time there are social formations which can be observed and described. Being clusters of social habits, these formations carry with them a notion of predictability, a potential for forecasting social behaviour. Among other things, social habits are the tracks through which information is processed. It can be posited that people who have acquired a certain type of education have really just established a certain type of habitual social behaviour.

DIRECTED AND NON-DIRECTED SOCIAL TRANSFORMATION

Social transformation is a passionless word. It does not have the same halo of mystification as the word development. The word development is therefore deleted from the vocabulary in this book and it is considered more clear and fruitful to describe reality in terms of *social transformation*. However, we are not satisfied with this expression alone. Despite questionable capability, our human desire for *steermanship* emerges. We want to control, manage, steer or direct social transformation. That is the goal of all governments and the intention of governments in the Third World particularly. Although we try, we do not really control social transformation. Therefore, we cannot talk about controlled social transformation. On the other hand, there is social transformation which occurs without the interventions of government. It appears that the terms *directed social transformation* and *non-directed social transformation* can be used productively. *Directed* social transformation may naturally be attempted also by other agents than government officials, for example missionaries or local politicians. The concept of *non-directed* transformation has much of the connotation of the word *spontaneous*. Transformation is on-going. At best, we can influence its direction. Today's societies are in a more tumultuous process of transformation than ever before and we find ourselves unsuccessful in directing events. We do not quite understand what is happening to us. The chaos arises because we do not command a clear view of the words we use. We do not process information well. Maybe the solution is simpler than we think. You cannot wait for others to save the world, you have to do it yourself.

3
information is the
opposite of uncertainty

*' We are very much glad you bring boxes
of health to our village and many good
advice for our people to learn.
Because why are we glad?
We shall know very much certain about
good health and the happiness of no sickness.'*

*Village headman in Tungati,
Luwingu, Zambia*

TALKING FAST OR LISTENING WELL

Information is not communication. Information is only potential communication. We must use information in the right way in the right social context for communication to occur. Communication between people thrives
not on the ability to talk fast, as some mass-media prophets seem to think,
but on the ability to listen well. We do not communicate by cramming an
enormous quantity of 'information bits' together in a monologue, but by
being socially intelligent and capable of listening to what the other person
has in mind before we respond. It is so simple, and yet we fail continuously in our attempt to communicate because of an egocentric attitude.

QUALITY OF COMMUNICATION

The weather bulletin predicts rain today. This statement is meaningful,
i.e. represents information to B, only if B knows what a weather bulletin
is. When A states, 'Aflatoxin in groundnuts and maize is the cause of the
high incidence of liver disease in the village,' the statement may not represent information to B because B may not know what Aflatoxin is. The
quality of communication between A and B depends on A's ability to sense
what B knows already and vice versa. An egocentric attitude, the inability
to see reality from the viewpoint of others, is the biggest communication
barrier. Massive egocentrism is, in fact, a pitiable state of mind because
the beholder is, as it were, imprisoned by his own perceptions. He is incapable of empathy, i.e. understanding a point of view different from his
own cultural percepts.

This applies to our daily conversation, but nowhere is it more evident

28

than in a situation where cross-cultural communication is attempted, for example between a European doctor and a village woman or between an agricultural expert and a group of farmers.

INFORMATION AND MEANING

What is information? What does it do to people? How do people use information? These questions require answers before proceeding.

Let us retain the idea that information is the opposite of uncertainty and employ the simple colloquial meaning of the two words information and uncertainty.[9] Meaning is a concept much discussed by philosophers. It may be fruitful to reduce the concept of meaning to a question of information. If information is the opposite of uncertainty, it implies that information reduces uncertainty. This is a fundamental concept in modern information theory. Uncertainty is something we do not like and therefore try to reduce. We seek information actively.

A asks B, 'Is the boss coming to the office today?' If B answers, 'Yes, he is coming to the office at 10.30 a.m.', A will be quite certain he cannot go shopping during office hours. If B answers, 'No, he is not coming to the office today, he is in bed with a flu,' A will be quite certain he can take time off. However, if B answers, 'The boss has a meeting in town, but he may come any time,' A is left in uncertainty until the boss arrives and is not likely to take time off. This situation has a high degree of uncertainty for A because it contains so many possibilities. The boss may arrive in 15 minutes, 20 minutes, 30 minutes, 3 hours, 5 hours, etc. If four different events may occur in a given situation, we feel more uncertainty than if only two events may occur.

MEANING AND PROBABILITY

If C sends a cryptic telex to D, 'Arriving tomorrow kindly meet,' D is in a state of high uncertainty if there is alternative transportation of boat, bus, train and air flights to his city. If only bus and air flights are available, D is less uncertain. The more uneven the probability distribution of the possible events, the less uncertainty there is. If 80 per cent of the travellers to D's city arrive by air and 20 per cent by bus, D can be reasonably sure C will arrive by air. If the bus drivers announce a strike that day, D can be quite certain C will arrive by air. All events which reduce uncertainty are carriers of information.

INFORMATION CAN BE MEASURED

In this book, we shall use the concept of information in such a qualitative sense. However, it should be kept in mind that the productivity of the concept is in its potential to be quantified. We can measure how much information is processed in a given situation by a given person.[10] The unit of measurement is called an 'information bit'. It can be defined as the quantity of information which is at hand when the number of equally probable possibilities is reduced by half. This definition can be illustrated by a simple game.

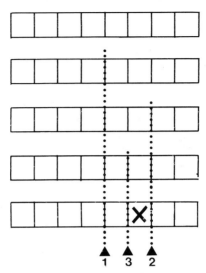

The task is to guess which square a person is thinking of. If the questioner divides the figure in half and asks: 'Is it to the left of the centre line?' — the answer will give one information bit whether it is yes or no. The number of alternatives (8) is reduced to half (4). We may say the uncertainty of the person guessing has been reduced by one bit. The questioner can continue the game by introducing a centre line through the remaining half of the figure, etc. It is easy to see that it takes three information bits to solve the problem which, conversely, means that the uncertainty to begin with was three information bits for the questioner.

The example illustrates a fundamental aspect of the way we process information in our daily lives. We seek information by continuously eliminating possibilities and evaluating probabilities. The example demonstrates also the two-value character of information. This 'binary code' is the fundamental trait of information processing both in our brain and in the computer. In other words, a computer, an individual or a social formation processes information simply by being responsive to *difference*, by continuously comparing the yes/no or current/no current impulses from reality. The purpose is self-correction for survival. Why should it be more complex than that? It may be useful for our understanding that we allow ourselves this simplistic explanation.

THE CONTEXT OF INFORMATION

One common characteristic of the small examples we have mentioned is that information does not occur in isolation. Information is information only as part of a larger context. Moreover, information itself is not in reality but in our mental or linguistic record of reality. We cannot extract information from events or objects themselves. We somehow always transform events and objects and this transformation is a simplification. We continuously edit information. Our minds would disintegrate in an information explosion if we did not have the mechanism of *selective perception*. There is nothing mystical about language. It is an invention which allows us to arrange information in a regular way so we can extract what we need and discard the rest. This is why sentences and not words are the essence of language. A word is only a thing representing another thing. A sentence is a model of reality demonstrating relationships between things and events. Language is a written or oral social habit formation facilitating our handling of reality with great economy. We organize reality, or shall we say our raw experience, into a consistent and readily communicable universe of ideas through the medium of a linguistic pattern. Without language, social formations are unthinkable.

THE INFORMATION PROGRAMME—A SERIES OF EVENTS

From our small examples, it is apparent that information is information only as part of a larger context. This larger context is termed a *programme*. A programme should not be mistaken for a language. With a language, we can construct an infinite number of programmes. Nor should we think of a programme in the narrow sense of a computer programme. Any social formation has a programme for its information processing, be it a television company or a beekeepers' association. A programme is simply 'a description of a series of events'. It just says that a number of events will take place in a certain order. As such, it is an attempt to forecast future events in reality. A programme is a description which a computer, an individual or a social formation uses to process information and to act upon it accordingly. This simple and comprehensible notion proves useful as we pursue the problem of directed social transformation. We do not ask the traumatic question *why* things or events happen. We simply ask *what* happens. A programme tells us what happens—or what will probably happen—and perhaps that is all we need to know. Many scientists have spent a lifetime trying to understand and prove causal relationships, whereas what they have achieved is the description of a series of events. Under the appearance of achieving exactness, why should we use words such as hypothesis, theory, model, method, classification system and others. In fact, the word *programme* will suffice.

The word hypothesis is a part of the contemporary scientific paradigm and may in future change as the paradigm itself changes. The words of scientific methodology represent no more than other words an absolute truth.

EVERYONE HAS AN INFORMATION PROGRAMME

Recognizing that a programme is an attempt to describe reality in memory, writing or any other tool of recording, it is obvious that others aside from scientists work with programmes. Scientists just give their programmes more complicated names than other people. All human beings or social formations work with preconceived ideas of reality and behave according to them. The Bemba farmer has a programme shaped by tradition and his own experience which prescribes the preparation of a *chitemene* garden. He has processed the available information in a way that makes him prepare the same garden in different places every year before the rainy season. Trees and shrubs are cut down in a circle about 50 or 60 metres in diameter so they fall with the top towards the centre. Once the vegetation is dry, the farmer burns it off. The ground is then cultivated with a hoe, mixing in the ashes. When the rains come, the farmer sows the garden with millet or cassava. In between the larger plants, he sows beans and lentils.

Under the circumstances of his environment, the Bemba farmer knows this programme for agriculture provides the biggest yield for his labour input. Until another programme proves to be more productive, this programme represents the least uncertainty and he will continue to use it.

When the owner of a small delicatessen in Copenhagen does his annual accounts, he has a programme for the procedure. He takes stock of his merchandise, establishes an inventory of his capital assets and calculates the depreciation, sums up the brute turn-over, deducts expenditures, etc. The programme which has set procedures provides the grocer with a high degree of certainty, unless, of course, he prefers another programme, i.e. that of engaging a chartered accountant.

When the Tollai tribesmen in Papua New Guinea take to the forest to trap wild pigs, they have a detailed programme for the venture. In their minds, reality is already described and they search the small narrow valleys where the pigs usually graze at a certain time of year. The Tollai know the pigs avoid the densest underbrush and follow certain trails. They know it is smartest to place the trap immediately after a bend in the trail. Ultimately, they know that if some of the band chase the pigs towards the traps and drive them down the valley, the results are achieved more quickly. The pig-hunting band of Tollai tribesmen is a social formation. Each man has a specific task to perform. The programme of this formation and the behaviour procedures for each man are described in detail in the memory of tribesmen. Under the circumstances, this programme provides the Tollai with a high degree of certainty.

ACTIVE OR PASSIVE PROGRAMMES

Usually a programme has an action objective. In that formulation, a programme is hypothetical in relation to reality. NASA is a social formation with a clearly defined programme of action in scientific research. Part of this programme was to let the Pioneer II spacecraft verify, or falsify, the hypothesis that life exists on Titan, Saturn's largest moon. Apparently, scientists have been preoccupied with Titan because it is slightly larger than the planet Mercury and has a thick atmosphere which may be similar to that of primitive earth. For example, spectroscopic readings by earthbound astronomers revealed that Titan's atmosphere is rich in methane gas, believed to be one of the primary ingredients in the earth's early atmosphere. The scientists hypothesized that, given the right temperatures, some forms of life or their precursors may have evolved on Titan. To test this hypothesis, the NASA scientists developed a highly complex computer programme of the reality of the solar system. This programme guided Pioneer II to its destination and allowed the scientists to control the venture with a high degree of certainty. Whether it is the Bemba farmer, the delicatessen owner, the Tollai tribesman or the NASA scientist, there is no difference in the way they process information. In each example, programmes are used as passive descriptions of events in reality or as descriptions of actions in reality for the purpose of reducing uncertainty. Also, in each example, behaviour is programmed in specific ways and the programmes are recorded in some kind of language. No refined distinctions are necessary regarding the perceptions of the information processing programmes by the respective individuals in the above examples. More germane to this discussion are the differences in the various languages which people use to record these programmes.

4
talking the same language and having time together

'How big is your house, Godson?'
Godson Handoma: *'I have house for my ancestors, the wife and God gave me eight children, Bwana.'*
'Yes, I understand that, but what is the size of your house?'
Godson Handoma: *'The house for my family is 15 paces, Bwana.'*
'How can a house be 15 paces, Godson? How long is a pace?'
Godson Handoma: *'The headman, Mr Viyambo, does the pacing in the village, Bwana.'*

'What surprises most is to find that various grand generalizations of the western world, such as time, velocity and matter, are not essential to the construction of a constant picture of the universe.'
B.L Whorf

COMMUNICATION—SHARING OF CONCEPTS

Sometimes in everyday life we use the expression: 'Mr Smith and Mr Jones do not speak the same language.' This does not mean that Mr Smith speaks German while Mr Jones speaks English. Rather it signals that Mr Smith and Mr Jones do not have much in common. Either they do not share views or they do not communicate well. Often we say to a person with whom we feel we communicate well, 'We should have some time together and talk,' or conversely, 'I have no time for him or her,' meaning that I really cannot communicate with that person, I do not like that person. We must assume that communication, and cross-cultural communication in particular, involves the sharing of concepts. Communication occurs when people have something in common. Therefore, when we want to understand the phenomenon of communication, it is essential to determine how people use language in similar or different ways. This concerns such fundamental concepts as time, space and matter, i.e. people's views of the world, the concepts they use to describe their daily reality and, ultimately, the universe. If languages differ, then the limits of a person's language also prescribe the limits of that person's world. However, it would not be of value to begin with a copious analysis of the scientific concepts which lead to the prolific technological progress in the industrialized countries or of the translucent philosophy of Confucius. Our concern is with the ways of people's everyday language.

METHODS OF MEASUREMENT

In Godson Handoma's village, the size of a house is not measured in square or cubic metres. A rectangular house is measured at the base by pacing one side and then pacing the adjacent side and adding the two together. Godson Handoma's house of 15 paces was 10 + 5, measured in that way. The pacing is done before construction by a person of trust and authority in the presence of the owner/builder. For Godson's house, the village headman, who also approves the location, held the required status and authority.

How long is a pace? The question has no relevance; you do not need to know how long a pace is when you know the man who did the pacing and even saw him do it. In this method of measurement, no clear distinction is made of the spatial dimensions with which a Westerner describes objects in reality. In Swahili, a single word, *urefu*, denotes length, tallness, height, depth and distance. The measurement unit and the concept of measurement are not standard, but depend on the situation and the experience of the observer.

In Godson Handoma's method of measurement, there is no reference to width and length, much less to area, nor is there any logical reason why such a reference should exist. This method is perfectly functional and adequate for the purpose of his village.

The experiential quality of the fundamental concepts used to describe reality is expressed also in the Swahili word for weight. The word *uzito* not only denotes weight and heaviness, it also denotes difficulty, severity, depression, slowness and pregnancy. What an expressive power! The English word weight is flat by comparison.

COLOUR TERMS

Swahili speakers describe reality differently in other areas as well. Although Swahili has been influenced variously by Arabic, Portuguese and English, it is basically a Bantu language. Examples from Swahili, therefore, have some linguistic relevance to other Bantu languages in Africa. In English and other Indo-European languages, there are numerous highly differentiated terms for colours. In Swahili, there are only three basic adjectives, namely

a) *ekindu* = red in all shades and varieties, i.e. scarlet, purple, pink;

b) *eupe* = white of any shade which, in addition, means bright, clear, transparent, clean, pure; and

c) *eusi* = black of all shades including dark shades of blue, green and red. All other colours are expressed with reference to objects. *Rangi ya kunde* = colour of bean = brown. *Rangi ya samawati* = colour of heavens = blue. *Rangi ya majani* = colour of leaf = green, etc. If a Swahili speaker is asked to describe the colour he sees in a landscape, he has the terms available for doing so. His final interpretation of Swahili colour-reality will obviously be different from that of an English speaker. However, we should not let this mislead us to infer that Swahili is a less sophisticated language than English.

Nyama = animal, meat and matter (substance). *Nyamafu* = dead animal. *Nyamaa* = stop talking, be silent, die away, cease, be still. The essence of the hunt and the survival is compressed in a single word. *Ota* = sprout, have a dream, sit by or squat down at. *Moto* = fire, zeal and ardour. Also, it means flames, marks on the body made by a stick. *Ota moto* = sit by the fire. That fire and dream is joined in one word is a vivid manifestation of the life around the fireplace.

LANGUAGE AND THOUGHT-ECONOMY

At a cursory glance, Swahili seems in some respects to have a less differentiated vocabulary than English. Should we assume, therefore, that English is a superior language? This is a common deception. All languages seem to be optimally functional and thought-economical about the reality they describe. In other words, a language used in a certain reality will always be the most rational way of processing information about that reality.

Swahili has a single word, *mshipa*, which rather vaguely denotes minor organs of the body such as blood vessel, nerve, vein, artery, pain, ache, swelling. Mama Mukahamubwatu of Tongaland, who was 85 years old and spoke Swahili, knew the names of several hundred plants, roots and shrubs in the bush. It is significant that she knew the names of plants for which she had a use. Those for which she had no use, she had no name. Obviously, Mama Mukahamubwatu did not require highly differentiated names for internal organs and was, therefore, satisfied with the single word *mshipa*. People develop the language they need for processing information about their reality in a thought-economical way.

THE CONCEPTS OF TIME

In the example at the beginning of this chapter, we showed that space and objects are not necessarily perceived in a three-dimensional manner. A three-dimensional view is *not* universal. In addition, the fourth dimension or the time-concept is not universally perceived in the same manner.

In English and other Indo-European languages, there is a time division according to past, present and future through the conjugation of verbs. In their perceptions and conceptions of reality, Westerners naturally use this division. As this time division is integrated into their thought patterns,

Westerners consider it to be a universal phenomenon or reality. There is reason to think that this 'fact' is no more than a presumptuous linguistic picture.

How did it arise—this notion that time is a smooth-flowing continuum in which everything in the universe proceeds at an equal rate, out of a future through a present and into a past? Or, to reverse the picture, where the observer is being carried in the stream of duration continuously away from a past and into a future.[11] Or, where the observer is standing in the present with the past behind him and the future in front of him. Time is perceived as an endless stream of time units. Westerners allocate a *pro rata* value to time. One piece of time is worth the same as another piece of time. On this basis, we calculate the value of work in man-hours. We make estimates of the future and records and accounts of the past. We use calendars, time graphs or clocks which are dismembering the experience of time in an endless row or circle of time-units. Time is chopped up like a sausage and sold by the hectogram because time is money. Westerners are buying and selling time but have lost the sense of time as a social value in the realm of human experience.

THE PSYCHOLOGY OF SITTING

The result is that people in western civilizations no longer have time for each other, they have no time together, they do not share the experience of time. This explains why Westerners are incapable of understanding the psychology of sitting. In villages all over the world, sitting is an important social activity. Sitting is not a 'waste of time' nor is it a manifestation of laziness. Sitting is having time together, time to cultivate social relations.

EVENT-TIME

Clock-time is one way of measuring time; another way is event-time. In villages all over the world, people are measuring time by events. Although the odd clock or wristwatch is evident, they function often as a prestige object. Measurement of time by the clock has no role to play and there is, moreover, no logical reason why it should. Women begin the day's work by judging the stage of the light. Even with seasonal variations in the light, it is usually an accurate assessment.

Then there is the time for sweeping, the time for weeding, the time for collecting firewood or carrying water, the time for pounding and preparing the main meal. Village life has a very set, daily routine. The various events in this routine are the 'points in time' in relation to which other events are judged. A farmer would say to a field worker, 'We may have the meeting after coming from the fields.' A woman would say 'after weeding time' or 'I will go to the clinic after sweeping.' Tonga herdsboys in Zambia measure time in relation to taking the herd to the water-hole, which they do daily at noon.

Africa, Asia or Latin America, whatever the language and culture, the measuring of time in relation to events is an almost universal trait in village life. Beyond the daily routine, the important event is the reference point. When was your son born, Mulenga? 'My son was born two rainy seasons after the great drought.' Bana Enifa, when did your husband leave for the Copperbelt? 'He left three moons after the death of the village headman.'

The tribal legends and folk tales are also peppered with references to the important events which function as 'historic dates'. For example, 'My father Sekeletu was a famous lion killer. He killed his first lion as a young boy the year Paramount Chief Lewanika of the Lozi died . . .' Or there is the tale of 'a famous singer in Gamu Gofa. His name was Tilahun and he lived in Arba Minch. He played his masinko and sang beautifully at feasts and weddings. Once he even sang for Emperor Menelik. The story I shall tell you now happened just before the battle of Adua . . .' People continuously construct time-scales on which the smaller events are measured as happening *before* or *after* the larger events.

THE QUALITY OF TIME

In a sense, time only exists when it is experienced. Hence the intensity, dominance or quality of an event makes that event the reference point for the passing of time. There is a deep rationale underlying that idea. If time is not experienced, it is of no interest. In the African village, or in other villages throughout the world, it is simply non-sensical to say, 'I do not have time.' If we consider time as experience, we can understand that in a world where there were no events, no change, there would be no 'time' either. It is notable in Swahili that there are double meanings to the words that come closest to the English words minute and second. *Dakika* is used for the sixtieth part of an hour, the minute, but it is also used to mean any small division of time. *Nusu dakika* corresponds to a second, but it really means 'a fraction or part of a minute'. Literally translated, it means half-minute. These words express a time-experience or a conception of the measurement of time which bears investigation. This time-concept becomes clearer in reference to the concepts of past, present and future.

TIME PASSED AND TIME EXPERIENCED

Zamani is a very value-loaded and important word in Swahili. Although it means the past, ancient times, antiquity, it also denotes time period or epoch. *Sasa* signifies the present, now, at this time, etc. Nevertheless, when using the expression 'nowadays', one would say *zamani hizi*, and for the expression 'our own times' *zamani zetu*. The past and the present mingle and the future is expressed by the word *baadaye*, which means thereafter, afterwards or next. The future does not exist because the events necessary for its human comprehension have not yet taken place.[12] Time is comprehensible only when it is experienced. It is judged by its content. Consequently, the notion of a future is almost without meaning, and the western concept of future as an *eternal continuum* in front of the human mind particularly has no relevance. There are no words to express this concept of future. In fact, some East African languages seem to be lacking a tense for a future which extends more than a few months. Eternity is not ahead of man. On the contrary, it is 'behind' him in *zamani*, the bygone which stretches indefinitely backwards yet forms part of the present. In the context of such a world view, it is obviously meaningless to utter the typical western expression 'You must have faith in the future.'

MEMORY OF EVENTS

For the individual, *sasa* and *zamani* have important implications. *Sasa*, the present, is considered the most meaningful because the individual has a personal memory of the events in it. Accordingly, one meets the idea that *sasa* varies with a person's age. The older a man is the longer is his *sasa*. *Sasa* disappears in *zamani*; the two concepts are intertwined. It is as if time is a loop which comes from *zamani*, passes into *sasa* in an arc, returning once again to *zamani*. This concept of time is very different from the western notion of a linear time continuum. In other words, *sasa* is a stream of duration which moves towards *zamani*. Certainly, there is a clear sense for the passing of the year with the rhythmic events of day and night, the months and the seasons, often with no feeling that this rhythm might cease. Essentially, the rhythm of life is perpetuated through the events of birth, marriage, reproduction and death. Birth is a slow process not concluded by the physical birth, but by the 'coming out' of the initiation ceremony. By the same token, death is a movement away from *sasa* into *zamani*.

TO BE LIVING-DEAD

Mohamad Farah told me his father was an *mzimu*, a spirit. When I asked about his uncle, he was *mfu*—just dead. A variant of the word *mzimu*, i.e. *mzima* or *uzima*, means in good health, full of life and vigour. *Mzimu*, therefore, has the paradoxical meaning of a 'living-dead' or a dead person who is still alive, whereas *mfu* means dead as a stone.

Mohamad's father had died recently, but his uncle died long ago. After the physical death, the individual continues to exist in *sasa* as *mzimu* as long as he is remembered by relatives and friends who outlive him. However, when the last living person to remember him also dies, then Mohamad's father passes into *zamani*. He is no longer *mzimu* but *mfu*. In other words, as long as a 'memory-picture' of a person remains in the heads of relatives and friends, that person is alive. This is not superstition on behalf of Mohamad, but behaviour according to the workings of the human mind. Mohamad's behaviour is consistent when he seeks the com-

pany of his father's *mzimu* several times a week and offers him food. Mohamad brings this food for his father's *mzimu* to the shade of a particular
tree. Although this tree is not exactly the abode of his father's *mzimu*
(which can be many places), Mohamad has selected it as a convenient
meeting place which they both prefer. The time-concept described above
has several practical implications for cross-cultural communication, which
will be referred to in a later context.

TIME, MIND AND HEART

Linguistic studies among the Hopi Indians in North America reveal a lack
of time divisions similar to the Swahili language.[13] In the Hopi language,
there is no such thing as a time-concept. There is no word for 'time' in a
western sense and the speakers of Hopi communicate efficiently without
conjugating verbs according to past, present and future tenses. The two
grand interrelated concepts in the world view of western cultures are time
and space. In the Hopi culture, there are two other concepts in the information processing programme. These are best described by the expressions *manifested objective* and *manifesting subjective*. The first comprises all events and objects that are or have been accessible to the senses.
The concept does not attempt to distinguish between present or past and
the future is totally excluded. The concept of the manifesting subjective
comprises everything we call future, including at the same time everything we call mental, i.e. everything that exists in the mind. This is an extremely logical combination since the future, indeed, can exist only in the
mind of a man being in the present. The Hopi do not use the term mind,
but a term more akin to our word 'heart'. It is worth noting that the word
moyo in Swahili may mean heart, soul, will and mind. The Hopi concept
of the manifesting subjective seems to derive from the extraordinary
ability man has to communicate with—and even control—the memory
pictures of people, objects or events in his own head. It is legitimate to believe that such communication can be facilitated through prayer and exer-
cises.

LIVING IS HOPING

The manifesting subjective, the 'heart' manifesting itself among the
objects and events of the outer world through practical action or prayer, is
expressed in the Hopi word *tunatya*, which corresponds most closely to
our word 'hope'. Man's attempt to manifest himself in this world can
hardly be more precisely expressed. Living is fundamentally an activity of
hoping. Like the western word 'time', the Hopi word *tunatya* is a key concept in an attempt to describe the world, to create a programme for processing information about reality. In the turmoil of our time, it is still un-
proven that the western concept yields the deepest insights. To dismiss as
mysticism the concept formations of other cultures may be lethal. As an-

other example, a brilliant demonstration of deductive thought is displayed by an aborigine tribesman. After tracking a wounded kangaroo, hear him explain why he interprets the signs a certain way—but there is no word in his language for time as an abstract concept. After 10,000 years in an almost unchanging environment, he has no use for it. Absence of change means certainty of expectation and an understanding of continuity in the concrete rather than the abstract.[14] The universe may be described in an infinite number of ways. The Newtonian concepts of space, time and matter are not universal, but are derivations from a certain type of culture and a certain kind of language. Newton did not find these concepts in reality but in the language.[15] He started the development of a programme for processing information about our physical reality which was later consolidated by Einstein, Bohr *et al.* In view of the apparent success of this programme, at least in certain areas of life, we may ask in what respect does it differ from that of the Swahili, the Hopi or any other culture, and what are the characteristics of this difference?

CULTURE IS LANGUAGE

It is imperative to demystify the word culture and recognize it simply as the language in which people structure their experience so they can communicate information from person to person. Further to this definition, it should be recognized that there may be differences between languages which are predominantly oral, such as Hopi, Swahili or other Bantu languages, and languages which are written, such as English or other Indo-European languages. With regard to very basic concepts, we do not share the same definitions. Written languages, by the very characteristic of being written, allow us through our western linear conceptualization of time to treat time as an object of the present. Here and now, we are enabled to record the past and schedule the future. The differences between oral and written languages require further clarification for the development of meaningful cross-cultural communication.

Sitting is not inactivity or inefficiency, not even sitting alone. Sooner or later someone going to town will pass by, bringing a message to sister Nakulu in Ndola that
she must send a message to husband Kubalula in Chingola to return home before
the rainy season to repair the roof.

In African cultures, one of the highest values is placed on the art of socializing. Here, civil servants are playing *Nsolo* during a lunch break in Lusaka, Zambia. *Nsolo* is an ancient board game based on the movement of counters according to certain rules. It requires analytical powers and the ability to draw fast conclusions from the opponent's moves. *Nsolo* is an abstract game requiring sophisticated formal logical skills.

5
into the archaeology of man's mind

'Midwife of health centre has many village midwives for help who cannot read books. I teach them coins to send with messenger. Wooden coin with one line across means birthing woman in 1 stage labour. Coin with two lines across means 2 stage labour. Yellow coin means difficult labour. Red coin means haemorrhage, rupture, bleeding. Then midwife of health centre come quickly to help village midwife.'
Siama Yuma, midwife tutor, Sudan

BEANS IN A BOWL

Ato Kassaye Negash is the name of a tenant farmer near Kambolcha in Welo Province, Ethiopia, if he is still alive. Ato Kassaye cannot read or write, or reckon. For him, objects are mostly two or three, or in extraordinary cases up to ten. Beyond that he thinks in concepts such as 'much', 'many' or 'enough'. His store house is built of *chicka* (mud) to a traditional size and he knows that if the storehouse is full in the autumn, he has 'enough' food till the next harvest. This concept of 'enough' is perfectly adequate for his purpose. His real problem is that there is hardly ever 'enough' food. For reasons unknown to Ato Kassaye, the agricultural extension worker wanted to have exact figures for his crop. He wanted to know how many goatskin bags of grain Ato Kassaye carried from the threshing place to the storehouse. Ato Kassaye is inventive. For every bag he emptied in the storehouse, he placed a red bean in a small bowl. He carried many bags and placed one bean after another in the bowl, so that the agricultural extension worker ultimately could count how many bags he had carried to the storehouse. After a while, when Ato Kassaye came to put a new bean in the bowl, he discovered all the other beans were gone. His arithmetic had been eaten by the cunning birds. You never win when all the odds are against you.

'Sheraf, how big is Acmajid Asha's herd?'

'Acmajid Asha is the richest nomad in El Obeid, sir. No people ask the richness of Acmajid Asha, sir.'

'Oh, I see, but how many cattle and how many sheep do you think he has?'

'Acmajid Asha has a small basket, sir, with small stones for sheep and goats and bigger stones for cattle.'

'I see, and what does he do with that basket, Sheraf?'

'When Acmajid Asha slaughters a sheep, he takes out a small stone, sir.'

'And what does he do when a lamb is born?'

'When a lamb is born, Acmajid Asha puts a new small stone in his basket, sir.'

SHAPING THE CLAY

Siama Yuma, Kassaye Negash and Acmajid Asha demonstrate something important to us in the way they solve practical problems in their lives. There may be something to discover about man's mind if we observe carefully the simplest and most evident ways in which he relates to and uses the objects in his reality. We should not trust his truisms, but rather marvel at man's ingenuity.

One day I met little Nalulu in a small village outside Chipata in Zambia. 'Are you helping your mother make clay pots, Nalulu?'

'Yes, I help.'

'And what are you making, what are these pieces of clay in a row?'

Nalulu (pointing): 'This is my brother.'

'And this?'

'This is my brother Suzgo.'

'And these two pieces?'

'This is Suzana and Luisa.'

'Oh, I see, you are very good at making clay dolls. So, how many sisters and brothers do you have, Nalulu?'

'I have two brothers and two sisters.'

'How many children are there in your family, then?'

Nalulu, counting the clay dolls: 'Four children.'

'Are you sure you are four children? What about yourself?'

Nalulu (looking down): 'We are five children, sir.'

Perhaps it is significant that as the human mind perceives objects in reality, it is often oblivious to its own presence.

To know more about man's intellectual and spiritual development, we should turn not only to the words, but also to the things, the objects of his attention. Of particular importance is *clay*, the object which most willingly yields to our desire to manifest ourselves and control reality. The earthenware potsherd may be of greater importance for the understanding of man's mind than the IQ test. It must have been a joyous experience for man the first time he passed a river bed or an incline where clay was exposed. He felt its softness under his foot, bent down and lifted a lump in his hand. Or, perhaps, it was a woman. She handled and fondled the object which responded so readily to the slightest pressure of her fingers. She discovered she could *shape*. It must have happened so long ago that people had no names yet for the trees, the moon, the sun, the rain, the grass. Or maybe it was at the time when they no longer carried their shelter to the water-hole, but the woman carried water to the shelter. They had settled for the night on the grass plains where seeds and fruits were plentiful. The woman held the lump of clay in her left hand. She kneaded it between her fingers, pressed the clenched fist of her right hand into it, turned the hand around and discovered she could make a hollow in the lump of clay. She did this several times with several lumps and threw them away on the sunny river bank. One day she came back and discovered the lump of clay with the hollow had hardened. She found her fingers could no longer shape it. She knocked at the lump with her knuckles and lost it in the shallow water. She took it up again and discovered that the hollow held water. She laughed in delight, lifted the first jar to her head, and began the task she has toiled with to this day.

TRANSFORMATION, THE SERVICE OF THE OBJECT

Over the centuries, the woman's ability to shape clay was developed. The technique of the turntable was discovered and various methods of firing the clay. These discoveries must have been accompanied by the delight of subjugating an object to obedient service. Archaeological sites overflow with the evidence of the potsherd—but these are the more conspicuous features of the period of unrecorded history. Of greater interest would be the thinking behind the hand that shaped the clay.

Thinking may be seen very simply as the action of inner hands shaping perceptions into concepts; as clay pots carry water, concepts carry information. When woman first shaped clay, she must have experienced the joy of transforming a piece of reality into the shape of another piece of reality. The joy must have been no less when woman discovered she could transform a lump of clay into the shape of a picture she carried in her head. She started producing art. Imagine her elation, that day so long ago, when she discovered she could shape a piece of clay as a goat. When she said to herself that the clay goat in front of her *was the same as* the goat she had grazing in the field. She made the first symbolic representation, the first abstraction. She made as many clay goats as she had goats grazing in the field and said, 'This is my herd of goats. There are as many clay goats as there are goats in my field.' Later, she realized that a piece of clay of *any shape* or a small stone *corresponded* to a goat in her field.

THE FIRST MODEL OF REALITY

This is the point at which *symbolic representation* was discovered, the notion that a thing can be made to represent something other than itself. The herd of goats in clay was, perhaps, the first *model of reality*. It may be just as simple as that. As the tools, the hoe and the axe, are inventions in the history of social evolution, so symbolic representation is a tool that was invented.

The episodes I experienced with midwife Siama Yuma, farmer Kassaye Negash, nomad Acmajid Asha and little Nakulu each in their own way illustrate this point. To understand the process of social transformation and the underlying process of people's mental development towards literacy, we must begin with the origin of symbolic representation and attempt to understand its evolution.

In recent decades, particularly in the Middle East, archaeologists have been piecing together several lost pages from the first chapters in the history of western civilizations. By now it should be no surprise to find that these pages are of clay. There is little doubt that the enormous social transformations of western cultures are linked to the extraordinary social phenomenon which we call the written language. How, when and why, was the written language invented?

WHEN WAS WRITING INVENTED?

Historically, it appears that two distinctly different types of writing emerged. The Egyptians and the Mayas of Mexico used pictographic writing systems in which each concept or word was represented by a miniature picture or logogram. This was a simple way of processing information. In terms of abstraction, cuneiform writing characterized by signs representing sounds was a more complex writing system in use as early as 5000BC. Later, the Greek and Latin alphabets evolved with letters that were phonogrammic, that is they represented sounds instead of objects. This system survived because it proved to be much more economical and convenient in processing information compared to pictographic systems. As societies using pictographic systems grew in complexity and sophistication, there was a need to construct arsenals of pictograms which could process such complex information. Finally, these writing systems consisted of several thousand signs and became unwieldy to use. Somewhere, sometime, there was an unknown genius who had the idea that signs could also represent the sounds he made when he uttered words. In this way, writing as we know it was born. A system with an alphabet of only 20 to 30 signs proved superior. Within the frames of a coherent grammar, writing based on a phonogrammic alphabet was capable of processing information in an infinite number of combinations. Although scholars have long believed that there was a direct evolution from the pictographic type of writing to the phonogrammic, they have been unable to trace the connections. It is likely that this evolution happened another way. Before investigating this, however, we should acquire a feeling for the epoch and cultures in which writing, as we know it, first emerged.

I am here mainly thinking about the evolution of writing in the Middle East area, since the important achievements of the cultures in, for example, China or India would provide us with another story.

A HISTORY OF TRADING

The Early Bronze Age, 3000—2000BC, seems to have been a formative period for the written cultures—although writing probably emerged as early as 5000BC. During this period, the golden triangle of land between the Euphrates and Tigris rivers and the adjacent provinces were dominated by warring city states and small kingdoms. The irrigated land was fertile and intense economic activity was taking place through the entire Middle East. Far-flung trade was a way of life and, as archaeology testifies from the layers of ruins, a tenacious bone of contention. Caravans criss-crossed the countryside, freighting metal from as far as Anatolia (now Turkey) and cedar wood from the forests of the present Syria to the prosperous city states in the golden triangle.

Cattle and agricultural produce made up only part of the goods for barter. The cities had craftsmen and women who produced fine merchandise in clay, wood, cloth and metal. They were capable of making refined intarsia furniture, gold jewellery and delicately woven cloth.

For almost 1,000 years, the people of Sumer made their imprint on the area with their language and writing system. Their sexagesimal mathematics is the basis of our 360 degree circle and 60-minute hour. From that epoch, other city states of renown are Sodom, Gomorrah, Gaza, Berytus, Babylon and Ur. Less well-known are the cities of Mari, Akkad and Ebla.

LARGE URBAN CENTRES

These walled city-fortresses with suburbs and neighbouring villages could comprise over 250,000 people. As many as 10,000 to 15,000 constituted a bureaucracy of civil servants who sustained the king and the ruling class. Already the human settlement phenomenon of the city appeared to prove that productivity and profitability are linked to the physical condition of spatial closeness of labour and the means of production. Then, as now, the phenomenon of economic expansion (more appropriately termed capitalist greed?) was the driving force in man's conquest and oppression of his fellow man. Control of trade routes, sources of raw materials and means of production were vital for the survival and expansion of these city states. Archaeological digs in the area show that these cities were burnt, ruined and rebuilt repeatedly within generations and the clay tablets tell stories of ferocious killing and arson, exaction of tributes from the conquered, and the signing of treaties with foes of equal strength.

From this background of undisputed cultural diversity and achievement, which coexisted with incredible bestiality and greed, three of the world religions—Islam, Christianity and Judaism—emerged into the world arena. These religions were probably part of a general trend to centralize power: all three centralize authority through monotheism and patriarchy. Considering the divisiveness and wars which characterize this period, the psychological appeal of monotheism and godsent saviours is understandable.

From the history of science and technology, we know that when people confront practical or economic problems they invent gadgets or methods which provide solutions. Writing is such a gadget, it is not imbued with mystery. Quite simply, it is a technological innovation for processing information.

RECORDS OF ECONOMIC TRANSACTIONS

When the trading caravan of donkeys set out on a month's journey to deliver 12 bags of grain, 5 clay pots of dried figs and 20 rolls of cloth, how could the merchant know whether the goods survived the adversities of the journey or the possible dishonesty of the donkey-drivers? How could the recipient know whether the quantities and goods delivered were correct?

The purveyor issued with the caravan a 'bill of lading' on a dried or fired clay tablet, with signs for bags of grain, pots of figs and rolls of cloth, as well as signs signifying the amount sent. In terms of information, this provided the recipient with certainty of correct delivery. If he sent the merchant a receipt containing similar signs, the sale was verified. Payment of salaries to the city bureaucrats and the army, land dealings, and collection of tributes and taxes from vassal villages were other economic transactions that required a reliable system of recording.

Writing was initially invented to solve the practical problem of recording economic transactions and, for a long time, it was probably limited to that function. As the social and economic life of the cities became more complex, however, other areas developed which required records, for example trade and peace treaties with rival cities. Man responded by inventing more sophisticated writing systems. At least in the Middle East, this may be considered the background for the evolution of writing.

THE POWERFUL SCRIBES

With the specialized skill of writing, the scribes became important men, almost as powerful as the king or the generals. They formed a highly esteemed and coveted class of professionals. In old Sumer there was an academy for scribes. The clay tablets reveal that scribes travelled widely in the Middle East, offering their services to rulers and merchants. Literacy was not for the layman. Then, as now, information was power, and the art of writing was like the many later technological innovations used by a few to control and exploit the masses. The scribes guarded jealously their professional influence in economics and politics. Their position of power was accentuated by the fact that the rulers in such times of unrest were the capable soldiers and ruthless killers who were usually illiterate. The kings were totally dependent on the scribes for formulating treaties with other sovereigns, issuing decrees to the armies, making laws for the people, collecting taxes and institutionalizing royal privileges.

In terms of information storage, the records on the clay tablets were infinitely superior to memory. Disagreements regarding land deals or cattle transactions were settled when the scribe read what was written. For common people, these mysterious signs in clay corrected memory inaccuracy. The efficiency of information processing was improved as if by a miracle. Orders could be sent over long distances and executed with exactness. Messages with the power to alter destinies could be sent to friends or foes in far-away lands.

INFALLIBILITY OF SCRIPTURES

In this turbulent climate of economic expansion and sudden doom, made more politically complex by the subtle manipulations of the scribes, it is easy to see why the written word was accorded godlike qualities. The notion of the infallibility of the scriptures arose. And this myth has been a source of enigma ever since. Similarly, during the emergence of the natural sciences, the myth arose of the infallibility of the scientific method and the sacredness of academia and its language.

HOW WAS WRITING INVENTED?

For our investigation we asked the question: 'How, when and why was the written language invented?' We have outlined an answer to why and have touched on when. Now we shall take a closer look at how. We return to the story of farmer Kassaye Negash and the red beans he put in a bowl to keep count of the goatskin bags of grain he carried to his granary. It may have been an innovation he introduced on the spur of the moment or a method he had observed used by others. This example elucidates the simple observation that, when we handle objects with our two hands, it is so natural to play a game and say to ourselves that objects outside our grasp are no longer outside when we replace them with objects which are inside our grasp. Objects outside the grasp of our hands have always been a problem to us, that is why we develop concepts in our brain with which to grasp them.

PEBBLES OF CLAY

As mentioned, writing had probably emerged by 5000BC as a response to the need for recording economic transactions. Trade and bartering had been important activities long before that point in time, however. So what did people use then to record such transactions—if anything?

Archaeologists have long been puzzled by the numerous finds of 'pebbles' on Middle East sites. These pebbles are small cones, discs, rods, spheres, etc. mostly of fired clay. Sizes vary from 0.5 to 1.5 centimetres and their various shapes and sizes suggest that they have been moulded between finger tips or the palms of the hands. Some of the pebbles have diametrical incisions, punched holes or similar markings. They have been found in more or less uniform shapes in sites from Turkey in the West to

Iran in the East and Sudan in the South. Dating of some finds is from 9000BC. Evidently, the pebbles were used for some purpose for the time span of 4,000 years before writing came into use. Several questions arise. Does the wide distribution and uniformity of the pebbles indicate that they had anything to do with trade? Were they simply used as counters? Did people in that distant past play the same counting game with pebbles as Kassaye Negash attempted with his beans in a bowl and Acmajid Asha with the small stones in a basket? If so, how did such a system of recording relate to the system of writing, as it later emerged?

WRITING ORIGINATED FROM RECKONING

A young scholar, Denise Schmandt-Besserat, specializing in the archaeology of the Middle East, has collected convincing evidence for a theory that writing has its origins in an archaic system of recording and reckoning.[16]

Among archaeologists, it has long been known that some of the abstract signs which remain undeciphered on ancient clay tablets must have been symbols for various commodities. Precisely which commodities the signs represented is not important: a circle with a cross may have represented a sheep, a cone may have represented a clay jar of beer, etc. It is the origin of these abstract signs which has puzzled archaeologists. The probable explanation emerged in several steps. The pebbles had, on some occasions, been found with hollow clay balls which appeared to have the function of envelopes or containers for the pebbles. A find at Nuzi in Iraq dated 1500BC held special significance. It was a clay ball containing 48 pebbles and, dating from this period when writing existed, happened to have a unique inscription on its surface. It was a cuneiform inscription specifying what the 48 pebbles represented. The pebbles were referred to as *abnus*, which means counters, and they represented a herd of goats and sheep. Since the sum of the different animals specified added up to 48, there could be no doubt about this assumption. Other finds of cuneiform clay tablets at the Nuzi site indicate that the word *abnu* was often used in connection with the verbs 'transfer' or 'deposit'.[17] As frequently verified by the archaeologists, the clay tablets were administrative records. For example, a text might read: 'PN brought 23 sheep, but their *abnus* have not been transferred.'

It seems that the Palace of Nuzi kept records of its herds by means of these small counters. Each animal was represented by a small object of a certain shape—the *abnu*. These objects were deposited in a series of baskets or trays. If a lamb was slaughtered, its *abnu* was removed from its particular container. If a goat was born, an *abnu* was added to a container. A comprehensive recording system of this type is very probable. In principle, it is not very different from today's accounting system, in which numbers are moved from column to column. It is worth noting that the Nuzi system had not yet taken numbers into use. Representation was made on a one to one basis.

TOKENS IN HOLLOW CLAY BALLS

The clay balls, usually the size of tennis balls, were called *bulla* or *bullae*. A later discovery in Suza, presently in Iran, contributed to the understanding of their function. Several *bullae* dating from the second half of 4000BC were found in Suza. These *bullae*, now in the archives of Suza, are about 2,000 years older than the Nuzi *bulla*. The significance of this find is that the *bullae* sometimes were marked on the surface with signs corresponding exactly to the clay tokens they enveloped, whether the tokens were spheres, discs, cones, etc. It is more than likely that there was a relationship between the shape of the clay tokens and the shape of the abstract signs as they were used in the earliest forms of writing.[18] It was further assumed that a *bulla* represented a commercial transaction, probably a bill of lading. The tokens *(abnus)* represented commodities. When the merchant dispatched a consignment with the conveyor, the donkey caravan driver, he gathered clay tokens in appropriate shapes and numbers and sealed them in the *bulla* by firing the clay. The caravan driver was obliged to deliver the consignment to the recipient together with the *bulla*. When the commodities arrived, the recipient cracked the *bulla* and could verify the contents and amounts via the tokens. Authenticity was often guaranteed by the merchant's seal on the *bulla*. It is likely that the token/*abnu*/*bulla* system was part of a much larger system of recording based on clay tokens for the purpose of storage, trade or taxation. As archaeologists have found *abnus* dating as far back as 9000BC, the principle of this system for information processing was applied through the enormous timespan of 7,000 years—and before the written clay tablet appeared in approximately 2000BC.

FROM TOKEN TO SIGN

In this period, we can expect that the system evolved towards increased sophistication. Precipitating the final change from token to sign representation was the principle of thought-economy. After a period of time had elapsed and the users had practised the double-check of having token or *abnu* inside the sealed *bulla* and the corresponding sign for the token on the surface of the *bulla*, it occurred to the users that in terms of information processing the former was superfluous.[19] Once use of the tokens was discontinued, the spherical form of the *bulla* became unwieldy. A transformation took place to a convex or flat clay-tablet on which the markings henceforth were made. With some justification, we may speculate that the notion of a written text having a 'content' derives from the physical fact of the token in the *bulla*. The dichotomy of form and content, such a long-standing debate among philosophers, may have had a very simple origin. The significance of the *bulla* for the development of language may be that it provided the tokens with a syntactical frame that was physical, hence tactile.

THOUGHT-ECONOMY IN COUNTING

Considering the long time period of its use, it is likely that the token/*abnu* system had also made an evolution by the time the transformation from *bulla* to clay tablet had taken place. The relationship of one token for one sheep is the simplest form of representation. However, the system became more sophisticated and evidence indicates that it reached a level of abstraction where tokens and signs in fact represented numbers.[20] There was an evolution from clay token to *abnu* in the sense that the *abnu* became a counter. A cone is assumed to have stood for one and a sphere for ten. (In the sexagesimal system of the Sumerians, a large cone was 60 and a cone with a circular punch was 600.)

Such a development is understandable in terms of the practical demands of the commercial transaction. If a merchant dispatched 30 sheep, the sheep were evident for the recipient, and a token for sheep was unnecessary. The important thing for the contractors was the quantity. Under a system of one for one, this meant a *bulla* with 30 *abnus* was rather impractical. Three *abnus*, each representing ten, proved to be a rational alternative.

THE ABSTRACT ABNU

At this stage in our description, we can provide an explanation of the non-pictorial, abstract nature of the writing on the oldest clay tablets. Writing arose from reckoning. The abstract signs in the earliest writing evolved from abstractions of the *abnus*. This notion is the focal point in the theory which Denise Schmandt-Besserat has pieced together from the scattered evidence of decades of archaeological excavations.[21]

We shall not pursue the evolution of writing beyond this point. Nor shall we explore how writing might have evolved in a parallel manner in other cultures or in other materials. Instead, we shall again direct our attention to clay, our starting point, and the ability of woman and man to transform it.

TESTS OF TRANSFORMATION

Kapele Sichilindi was her charming name, and it made me even happier to hear that she was from a place called Chimbilimbili, but for the time being she lived with her husband in Chawama, a small human ant-hill of rusty corrugated-iron sheets, flattened cardboard boxes, stubs and other available remnants outside Lusaka. Kapele was a graceful being, given to laughter and quick in work, like a *dikdik* antelope. She had one small child on her back and one soon to be born. Kapele could not read or write, but she was very clever at working with clay. She sat all day long with other women kneading lumps of clay and turning them into beautiful pots on a crude turntable.

One day, I took two small lumps of clay and rolled them into balls between the palms of my hands. I gave them to Kapele, one in each hand, and asked her to 'weigh' them. 'Do you feel there is as much clay in that ball as in that ball?' Kapele disagreed. She said there was more clay in the ball in her left hand. Then I took a small piece of clay away from the ball in her left hand and rolled it smooth again. Kapele held one ball in each hand, 'weighing' them carefully, and decided that there were equal amounts of clay in both hands. After that, I asked her to take one of the balls and flatten it into a pancake. Kapele flattened it on the table so that in front of her lay a pancake and a ball. She studied them for a while, then looked at me, obviously expecting another question. 'Kapele, is there now more clay in the ball than in the pancake, or is there more clay in the pancake than in the ball? Or is there the same amount of clay in the pancake as there is in the ball?' Kapele was quite convinced there was now more clay in the pancake than in the ball. When I asked her why, she said, 'It *looks more* in the pancake.'

CONSERVATION OF MASS

According to one of J. Piaget's tests for assessment of conceptual development, Kapele had not established the concept *conservation of mass*.[22] She had not formed a logical structure by which she retained the idea of a 'logical necessity', i.e. *because* there was the same amount of clay in the two balls a moment earlier and because nothing had been removed or added in the process of making the pancake, there had to be the same amount in the pancake and the ball. Kapele was apparently more controlled by her perceptual field, by what she saw here and now, than by such a logical structure.

Together with my colleagues, I carried out many tests of this type with other people who did not read or write and the observations were often the same. Age had no bearing on the tests. People of 70 years or more also assessed quantity according to visual perception. As the reader will see from the pictures following this chapter, we also carried out tests to assess development of other concepts related to conservation of mass, such as conservation of quantity, conservation of numbers, the straight line, and horizontality. In a western culture, children have formed these concepts by seven to ten years of age. Many of the adults we tested in rural areas either had not formed the concepts or appeared to have a weak formation of them. For example, of 63 subjects tested for conservation of mass, 55 per cent answered incorrectly.[23]

Several inferences can be drawn from this experience. One is that commanding and understanding a language is not only a process of 'learning the meaning of words', but also the much deeper problem of mastering a conceptual technique which is an underlying and unpronounced feature in the language itself. Another inference is raised by asking: Why should people have formed concepts for which they have no use?

PIAGET—AN ETHNOCENTRIC DISTORTION

The conservation tests form the basis for Piaget's theory of mental development, a theory which is assumed to be universally applicable. This is another ethnocentric distortion. The theory may be valid for children raised in western cultures, but it should be apparent that conceptual development is culturally conditioned. For this reason, it is doubtful that tests of this kind, developed in a western setting, should be applied to an African milieu. Only the fact that Kapele was well acquainted with the physical properties of clay makes such a test permissible.

For the purpose of our continuing investigation, we will remember that the change of a clay ball into a pancake is a very fundamental example of a *transformation of an object.*

Archaeology has demonstrated the origin and development of writing to us. At the same time, it has revealed the physical connection between the object and our thought about the object. There is a concrete link between our thinking and the actions of our hands. To know is to transform and modify an object and to understand the process of this transformation. The essence of knowledge is action with our hands.

The experience with the Piaget tests forces us to rethink some basic assumptions and to re-evaluate our attempts in cross-cultural communication. The starting point in a western conceptual model may be wrong. Rather, we should begin with a search for other models. People in other cultures may have useful ways of communicating, of which we are unaware.

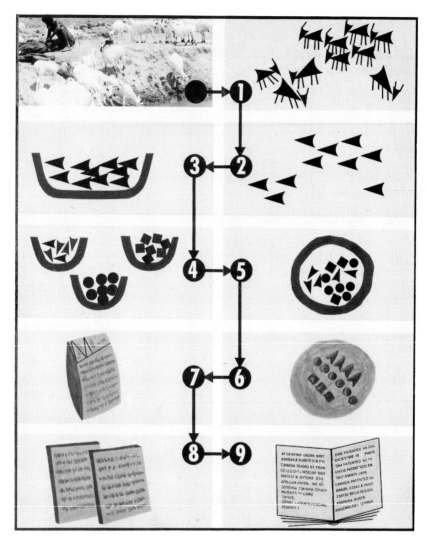

From reality to written language. 1. People discover that they can create the shape of one object in another object, clay. The concept is formed; the clay goat represents the real goat. 2. The clay goats are transformed into simpler, 'abstract' objects in clay pebbles. 3. The pebbles are kept in a basket or clay bowl. This is the context for the first concept of numbers. The clay tokens in the bowl 'correspond to' the herd of goats in the field. 4. The pebbles are transformed into a systematic set of counters, different shapes in different bowls; a system of accounting emerges. 5. The clay bowls are closed and made into hollow clay balls suitable for use as portable bills of lading. 6. The tokens inside the clay ball are also 'written' on its surface, thus leaving the contents superfluous. 7. The clay ball is collapsed to make the first pillow-shaped clay tablet with written signs. 8. The clay tablet becomes slimmer and the written signs more functional. 9. Paper replaces clay, the handwritten and later the printed book is invented.

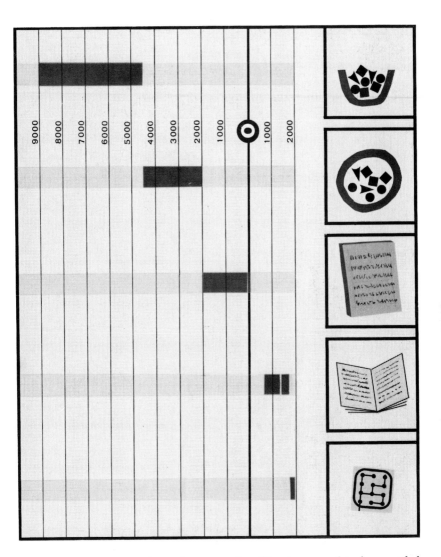

The quantum leaps in information processing. Man is assumed to have settled around the year 10000BC. Counters in the form of clay pebbles have been dated as far back as the year 9000BC. Clay balls *(bullae)* providing the pebbles with a context begin to appear in archaeological digs 5000—4000BC, and were probably in use for 2,000-3,000 years up to the period around 2000BC, when the dramatic transformation to abstract signs on clay tablets took place. Around the year AD700, development accelerates. The first bound, handwritten, paper books are the Irish gospels from the period AD 650—700. In 1456, Johann Gutenberg introduced the first printed Bible. The computer chip was invented in the 1960s. Presumably, there have been long overlaps in the stages. Most important is not exact dating, but the evident acceleration of the process.

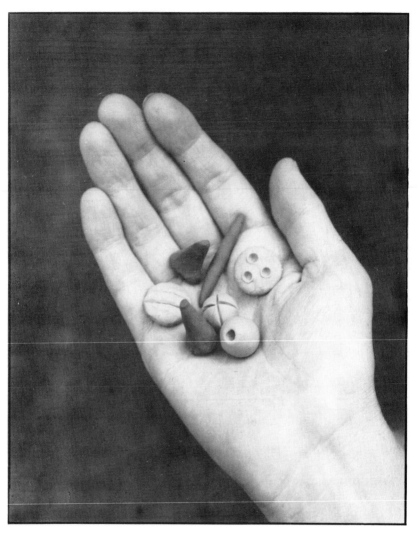

Models of some early clay tokens. Note how the forms are easy to shape between the fingertips. Indentations are easily made with a stylus.

Model of pillow-shaped tablet from Tell Harmal in Iraq. The tablet contains an algebraic-geometrical theorem similar to that of Euclid. It is datable to early 2000BC.

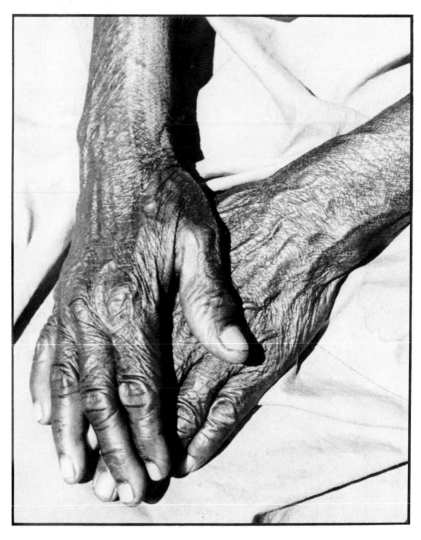

Our thoughts are more closely connected with the actions of our hands than we are aware. There is wisdom in people's hands.

There is more clay in the pancake.

. . . or there is more Fanta in the high glass. Why should we consider it 'less logical' to attribute 'moreness' to something visually dominant like width or height than to attribute 'sameness' to something invisible like weight?

We gave Kapele a handful of pebbles and asked her to show the shortest, quickest way to walk from one hut to another. The straight line is a social convention in a carpentered environment. In other environments, people may not have a use for it.

Show me how these trees grow on the ground. How do they grow on a hillside?
More than half of the people related verticality to the sloping hillside rather than
to the horizontal baseline.

Ten small pebbles in a row and ten larger ones. Each large pebble is married to a small pebble, each row contains the same. What happens when we move the small pebbles together in a short row? About 40 per cent of the people said there were more pebbles in the longest row.

Are such observations interesting—or are they misleading because we make judgements about people's competence based on cultural norms different from their own?

6
the word is just another thing

HONEY-CUCKOO—A CONCEPT

I have quoted the old Tonga woman before. In her language, *hamubwatu* means *he-who-drinks* and *Muka-hamubwatu* means *she-who-is-married-to-he-who-drinks*. This time she gave me the knowledge of how to get hold of a honey-comb. The honey-cuckoo has established a collaboration with people. The bird knows where the beehive is because it likes the larvae. So, if you follow it through the bush for long enough, you will find the hive. Then you gather dry grass and leaves and twist them into a torch which you light and hold under the hole of the hive. When the bees are numbed by the smoke, you crack open the hive. The honey-cuckoo can revel in larvae whilst you can take the honeycomb and sell it at the market in Choma!

A PROGRAMME FOR ACTION

To my mind, Mukahamubwatu's story is interesting not only for what it says, but also for the principle of knowledge that it displays. It is clearly an efficient form of information processing. It is practical information structured in a programme of action which is rewarding because it is based on a thorough experience.

The concept of the honey-cuckoo, from which the whole programme is derived, has quite definite boundaries. Immediately the concept is defined, a person knows where and when to go and what to do to get honey. To say a concept has definite boundaries is to say it gives us a high degree of certainty, it carries information. There is no reason to believe any principal difference exists between a practical concept like the honey-cuckoo and a scientific concept like gravity. However, there may be differences in the capacity of concepts to convey information. Some concepts do not carry information at all and may, therefore, appropriately be labelled quasiconcepts.

CONCEPT FORMATION

If we want to improve our performance in cross-cultural communication (for example in adult education and similar programmes), we need to know more about concepts. The question 'What is a concept?' would only lead us into another philosophic trauma. Rather, we should ask: What happens when concepts are formed? And more specifically: How are concepts formed in different cultures? Or perhaps: Are there differences in the ways concepts are formed in different cultures? Another useful question might be: How do we *use* the word concept?

In our investigation of the process of concept formation, we may be tempted to think that a difference should exist between the formation of concepts which are oral and the formation of concepts which are written. This may not be so. We should remember our experience from the previous chapter where we traced the evolution of the word from a piece of clay. Writing as we know it is a two-dimensional system of signs which evolved from a three-dimensional token/recording system. Writing is a human invention.

A CONCEPT IS SIMPLE

The scriptures are neither godsent nor infallible. The word is just another thing. If we agree with that statement, we may realize that there is no need to feel or believe that a concept—or rather the concept of a concept—is difficult to comprehend. Or, that it is a problem so profound that only philosophers and psychologists can grapple with it. When we define the boundary of an object, it becomes certain for us. It has a *certain form*. A concept is like an object which we handle with inner hands. It is a *logical form* which we can keep as it is or transform with our thoughts. When we handle these concepts in our heads, we process information and acquire certainty. Certainty is essential to survival.

OBJECT AND EVENT

When we attempt to describe our physical reality in a systematic manner in English, we talk about *objects* and *events*. By object, we mean in colloquial language a body or thing, something of permanence which is still there when we do not actually see it. More specifically, an object is characterized by a tangible, three-dimensional extension in space. In our daily language, an event is something other than an object. Events are perceived as a movement of something, a change or a happening in the time dimension. For practical reasons, we define such a distinction, which makes it easier and more convenient for us to cope with reality. On closer inspection, it is apparent that the distinction between an object and an event is really just a matter of the time-scale of our observation. An apple is an object today, but after a certain period of time it is perceived as an event. It rots and ultimately disappears completely. A piece of rock is an object today and probably in 5,000 years hence. In the perspective of two or three million years, the rock is an event. Nature will have transformed it completely. Our physical reality is only seemingly stable and permanent. It is as much in flux as our social environment, only at a different pace. Physical objects and social formations share the same feature of being in continuous transformation. We have not failed to observe and register these changes around us, which are often imperceptible, and this is reflected in our concept formation.

STORY BY THE FIRESIDE

Our brain is processing information out of a perceptual chaos by creating a conceptual order. To understand the emergence of language from a psychological vantage point, we must understand early man and woman's need to share experience in an environment alternatively hostile and kind. The *story* by the fireside was the mechanism for sharing experience. It is revealing that the Swahili word for 'story' and 'event' is the same: *kisa.* From the setting of the storytelling, we can understand how the language habits of the group in a large measure determine the group's conception of reality. As our hands are capable of transforming *concrete* objects, so our thoughts are capable of transforming *abstract* concepts. As always, habit formation facilitates this process.

WE OBJECTIFY

One such habit in English and other Indo-European languages is that we objectify events.[24] This is the reason why we make some events *fixed points* by calling them *objects.* The same applies when we, in a sense, hold firm *a continuous happening which we perceive* (which is not a thing) by putting the word *event* instead (which is a thing). Let us look at some practical examples. We objectify the time between sunrise and sunset by calling it a *day.* We even push our luck and talk about seven days just as we talk about seven stones in a row. This is extraordinary since seven stones can be clearly perceived, but seven days cannot be perceived. The day, *today,* can be perceived, at least to some extent, but the remaining six days *exist* purely in our imagination and cannot be perceived from anything in reality. This also illustrates how we use numbers. In both examples, we use the number *seven* with the same ease, although in the case of stones we are counting *on* each stone from one to seven, whereas in the case of days we have nothing *to count on.* The numbers are sort of *counting themselves* or, expressed another way, we have formed a language habit which assumes that we are counting on *something real.* We behave as if seven days were countable and then just go on counting them. In the same manner, we talk about *14 steps forward, 12 strokes of a bell, the ship sunk 30 nautical miles south-west of Lindesnes.* This is all pure imagery. We should be aware that in the early formation of language this was an exciting invention, a linguistic innovation which we later made into a habit. This linguistic innovation, which led to the development of abstract conceptualization, is probably a key to the emergence of science. These examples seem to indicate that language habits and concept formation are linked. Perhaps they are simply two sides of the same phenomenon.

TIME AS A TANGIBLE OBJECT

Earlier, we touched on the concept of time, how in western cultures we talk about *lengths of time, time units,* etc., proceeding to count and calculate with these units as if they were tangible objects. We also mentioned how *past, present and future* are related notions. This ability to objectify has been developed at the expense of our subjective experience of *duration*—the fundamental relation of *later* to *earlier.* We recall that in Swahili the word 'future', i.e. *baadaye,* means *later, afterwards* or *next.*

B. Lee Whorf reports how scores of other languages function efficiently with only two tenses corresponding to *later* and *earlier.*[25] In the Hopi language, the western *length of time* is not regarded as a length, rather it is a relation between two events in lateness. The Hopi language does not objectify. The Hopis have no language habit that cloaks the subjective experience of *becoming later.* As a consequence, an expression such as *seven days* literally cannot be used in such languages. The sentence 'My brother stayed seven days' would be equivalently expressed in an operational manner, as an event, 'My brother left after the seventh day.'

FORMING THE FORMLESS

Another aspect of our habit of objectifying in western languages is the way we manipulate the nouns for physical things. For objects with definite spatial outlines such as *a stone, a house, a bottle,* it is easily understood. These are individual nouns and we objectify *real objects.* We use mass nouns such as *water, air, wood, wine* in the same way, only without attributing a plural form. How do we objectify these *boundless extents?* We simply 'individualize the mass', by combining the formless item with an item with form—by saying, for example, *a cup of water, a piece of wood* or *a bottle of wine.* In that way, masses are easier to handle, i.e. *to think with.*

These examples of how we objectify in western languages say something important about our concept formation. To objectify means literally what it says, to make an object. In order to understand more completely the implications of such a proposition, we should return to the conception of an object. Let us put aside briefly our knowledge that an object is also an event. From direct experience we know that an object is something tangible and transformable. It forms an entity with coherence and spatial extension; at the same time, it is a collection of parts.

THE PRESENCE OF CONSTRAINTS

A table is a collection of four legs and a top. The point that makes the table more than a collection of parts is the presence of what we could call a *constraint.* For example, when the position of the three table legs is known, there is obviously a constraint for the position of the fourth leg, which is given by the position of the other three. The essence of the table being an object rather than a collection of independent parts is due to the presence of the constraint.

Constraints correspond to the conceptual boundaries referred to by Gottlob Frege. In terms of information processing, constraint means reduction of uncertainty. A world without constraints would be totally chaotic. Constraints mean predictability and are the means by which we create conceptual order. When we *define* the concept of a table, we create a new object—'concept table'—possessing *the same* constraints as the real object table. Then we can look at and *handle* the real object, table, through its replacement, the new object, *the concept of the table.* Our perceptual problem is that once we have defined a new concept we think that it constitutes something more than a new object. We want to understand something that is already in clear view and this is what we seem not to understand.[26] There are no *meanings* going through our minds except the concepts or the verbal expressions we have created. Our language *is* the vehicle of thought. The word is a thing—there is no better way of expressing this.

I KNOW—AN EXPRESSION OF CERTAINTY

How do we move then from thing to thought? Or is it necessary to ask this question at all? In what sense should thinking be more than perception? It could be just perceptions of descriptions of perceptions. When I look at a chair and somebody asks me: 'What do you see?' I say, as a matter of reporting, 'A chair.' I have climbed several flights of stairs and look into a room and exclaim, 'A chair!' Both my *report* and my *exclamation* are expressions of perceptional/visual experience. But the exclamation is so in a different sense from the report. The exclamation is forced from me. It is related to the visual experience as a cry is to pain.[27] Since my exclamation is a description of a perception, it can also be called the expression of thought. If I am looking at the object *chair,* I need not think of it, i.e. use *the concept of the chair.* But if I am expressing my visual experience in the exclamation 'A chair!' then I am also thinking of what I am seeing, i.e. I am using *the concept of the chair,* I am recognizing the constraints of *a chair,* I am processing information about the object 'chair'.

We should not make it difficult for ourselves by asking: What is knowledge? Rather, we should ask: In which situations do we use the expression, 'I know'? Mukahamubwatu tells me, 'You can find honey by following the honey-cuckoo.' I answer, 'Yes, I know that now.' My teacher tells me, 'The square root of nine is three.' I answer, 'Yes, I know.' In both situations, I simply signal a *feeling of certainty*. When I say 'I know', I simply say that an expression of uncertainty would be senseless in the situation. If there is a difference between experiential and mathematical certainty, we will not pursue it in this discussion. In Swahili, one of the words for knowledge is *hekima*. It also means wisdom and judgement as passed by a supreme authority. Mukahamubwatu is an elder in her village. Her *traditional knowledge* gives people a great *feeling of certainty*.

NO UNIVERSAL LOGIC

In the negation chair/not chair (either this is a chair or it is not a chair), I am certain there is no third possibility. That certainty exists only because, when I use this concept, I am unable to turn my attention away from the concept. If I did that, I would lose my *feeling of certainty*. What we call *logical necessity* is only an arbitrary linguistic rule that gives us a *feeling of certainty*. There cannot be a formal logic which is universal, i.e. which is valid for all cultures. So, how can there be a *knowledge* which is universally valid? Mukahamubwatu's knowledge is not inferior to that of a scientist.

WE LOOK FOR REPETITIVENESS

What is the nature of science? This is a common question. Why should science be different from any other way of searching for information? If we reduce scientific method to its essence, we can say it looks for the repetitive. A law of nature describes the repetitiveness of certain events. It is a law because it is a set of constraints. Let us investigate the basis in everyday language and experience for various concepts linked to the concept of repetitiveness. Words such as *regularity, cyclic, rhythmic, likeness* or *resemblance, predictability*, as well as *order, harmony, system* and *symmetry* may not be as different as they seem. It may be possible to trace their origins to the same experiential basis and thereby demystify them. Then, we may be able to eliminate such bombastic questions as: What is the nature of scentific knowledge? We seem to display a propensity for seeking complicated answers when a simple question is all that is necessary.

WE RESPOND TO DIFFERENCE

Like the computer, our brain responds to difference. We know this intuitively and do not really question it. Our senses register variation in stimulation and not static stimulation. From our environment, we process information in the most economical way through a perception which is highly selective. Our brain does not have the capacity to cope with all the information available in reality. It must select and register only the information likely to affect us. In a world of continuous transformation, we generally focus our attention on those transformations which are conspicuously important to our survival. We can experience this phenomenon through some very simple examples. Imagine certain configurations passing as in a film in front of you from left to right on the page. The oval represents your field of perception:

You will very quickly *learn* that there is no variation in this series of sticks passing through your perceptual field and you will turn your attention away from it. However, when you spot the occurrence of a difference

you immediately turn your attention to it in order to detect its possible significance. If this difference starts

occurring at intervals some interesting things happen. You start perceiving a *rhythm* in the impulses of the stimulation, a feeling that there is a *cyclic* movement in the happening. If the difference continues to occur, your memory,

MEMORY

which is that part of the series of impulses which has passed through your perceptual field, reinforces your here/now perception and you *learn* that certain impulses occur with *regularity*.

REGULARITY AND EXPECTATION

From the notion of regularity derives the notion that 'the same is going to happen later'.

EXPECTATION	PERCEPTION	MEMORY
(The Future)	HERE/NOW	(The Past)
	(The Present)	

It is this expectation, here/now, of what is going to happen later that forms the basis for the concept of *the future*. The starting point for all learning is the learning of such simple regularities. The baby gurgles with joy and grasps for the red ball, but if you hide the ball under the blanket, the baby behaves as if the ball had never existed. However, if you hide and show the ball in regular intervals, you will observe that the child develops the expectation of seeing the ball again.

PREDICTABILITY

We have said that science looks for the repetitive. Only from the notion that event A occurs regularly, i.e. from the expectation of A's recurrence, can we develop the concept of the *predictability* of A's occurrence. In terms of experience, there is no difference in principle between the expectation of the baby and the expectation of the scientist. Both are in a quest for the certainty of information. Man's concepts of *hope* and *fear* have grown into obese value distortions of his future. Strides could be made in our understanding of reality, if we began with the premise that the content of our daily conversation is based on pleasurable and displeasurable expectation.

Returning to our example of how the concept of regularity further influences our way of processing information, let us imagine that a pattern emerges in our series of impulses, such as:

| | |SSS| | |SSS| | |SSS| | |SSS·····▶

or other shapes, as:

●●●○○○○●●●○○○●●●○○○○·····▶

It is often said that in man's mind there is a drive towards *harmony* and *balance*. When we look at the examples, we would use precisely these two words to describe what we see in them. We feel intuitively that the examples provide the experiential basis for using words such as *order*, *system* or *symmetry*. The underlying factor here is our observation of what we call *likeness* or *resemblance*. In our perception is a tendency to organize elements in a whole on the basis of certain criteria, for example, the criterion of likeness. Intuitively, we group together elements which are similar to each other. We think of the whole as consisting of groups of repeated elements, as in the following:

| | | |SSS| | | |SSS| | |

or:

●●● |○○○ |●●● |○○○

Why does this phenomenon occur? It does not come naturally to us to think of the whole as consisting of irregularities:

| | |S |SS| | |S |SS   or: ●●●○ |○○ |●●●○ |○○

For some reason, people perceive as harmonious those elements with the same visual characteristics which are grouped together. We feel they 'belong to each other'. A similar phenomenon in our perception and way of processing information is the phenomenon which Gestalt psychologists call the 'good configuration'.[28]

We fill in or complete these curves and curve branches with the most *natural*, *harmonious* or *symmetrical* course of the lines:

This is what we *see*. We tend to perceive the curves extended into bounded fields, complete entities or *wholes*. We do not know whether this is a valid assumption for cultures having little or no pictorial tradition. Our formation of verbal concepts need not be more mystical than that. The same perceptual phenomenon applies to verbal conceptualization. A concept is not a concept unless it has boundaries, i.e. the constraints make the concept carry information.

PRINCIPLE OF PROXIMITY

The phenomenon just described is manifest not only in our visual perception but also in our perception process through other senses. The point is that such *wholes* are registered by our brain more easily, accurately and economically. Other evidence indicates that such *wholes* are easier to store in the memory. The examples described above all emerge from the fundamental and generally accepted psychological *principle of proximity*, i.e. sensory motor processes which take place simultaneously or in short sequence are perceptually organized in the same *whole*, so that one process has a tendency of producing the other—or producing the expectation of it.

ENCODING AND DECODING

This can be demonstrated by taking our example one step further:

$$OIIOIOIIOIOIIOIOIIOIOIIOI$$

Our tendency to organize individual phenomena, elements, characteristics or relations in larger *wholes* is synonymous with the term *encoding* in information theory.[29] The reverse function is called *decoding*. I ask you to remember the above row of two-value symbols so that you can reproduce it for me later. If you look at it and try to register each symbol one by one, 25 in all, you will discover that this far exceeds your brain capacity. However, if you group the symbols in sequences

$$IOIIO$$

you will quickly discover that the row contains this combination five times. This is precisely what happens by itself in the process of perception, making it possible for us to collect, store and retrieve large quantities of sensory information. In other words, we would process the information by encoding and decoding the formula '10110 by five'. Clearly this is an easy and very thought-economical way of storing and reproducing a row of 25 symbols.

ENCODING AND PROGRAMMING

Our encoding function thus utilizes what can be traced of regularity in the information. We now understand that this function relates to the concept of logical classification—a function to which the philosophers and psylogists have devoted considerable time without realizing that there is no such thing as a universal formal logic before Ludwig Wittgenstein called their attention to it. . We should also be aware that encoding is the core function in what we term the *programme* for the processing of information. As pointed out, encoding is not limited to visual stimulation or a written language; it takes place as well through the other senses, hearing, touch, taste or smell. Encoding is another word for the function of objectifying.

7
of course there are spirits

'. . . Then I talked to one of the elders in my village and he was a very old man, so I wanted to listen to him. He was 48 years old.'

James Digmai, Madang, PNG

'It is possible that some of the brain's miraculous properties—of showing foresight, intelligence, etc.—are miraculous only because we have not so far been able to observe the events in all the significant variables.'

W. Ross Ashby, Cybernetics

THE ELDERS ARE NOT SUPERSTITIOUS

People in industrialized countries have some distorted notions about the so-called traditional societies in Africa or elsewhere. One of them is that the elders obstruct and delay *modernization*. We should realize that the elders are, in fact, not so old and that we need to understand more about their special function. Another western preconception is that people's minds are controlled by all sorts of shady superstitions in the form of taboos and magic. Even a modest exploration of such social phenomena may give us a better understanding of them. Of course there are spirits in the villages. And, under certain social circumstances, miracles are perfectly normal happenings.

AGE GROUPS AND ELDERS

In very simplified terms, we can say that in western societies there is a tripartite division of age groups into children, youngsters, adults—with an almost cultic social attention accorded to youth and the youthful and, conversely, a badly concealed contempt for old age. In other societies, for example Bantu societies in Africa, the divisions have a different status emphasis and follow different lines: children, adults, elders. The group of adults is often subdivided into unmarried youngsters and married adults and great attention is given to the transformation of the individual from childhood to adulthood through initiation ceremonies, but the focus of social attention is clearly accorded to the elders. The elevated status of the elders can be understood in the context of the significant role they play in the function and survival of these societies.

In Swahili the tripartite expressions are *mtoto, kijana, mzee. Mtoto* means child and at the same time anything which is characterized as subordinate, extending even to the domain of such things as a trailer of a lorry. *Kijana* means youth, ranging from 'one who has passed seven years and has sense' to 'one who is in full vigour and capable of bearing arms'.

THE LIVING-DEAD AND THE SPIRITS

To become *mzee*, an elder, is to reach the desirable pinnacle of life, endowed with dignity, wisdom and power, and as importantly to exercise control over the vital material resources of the society such as food, cattle or land. It is significant that *mzee* not only means an elder, but also a parent and an ancestor.

In Chapter Four, we described the concept of the time-loop, in which the stream of duration passes from *zamani*—the past—through *sasa* —the present—and back again to *zamani*. Also touched on was the subsequent belief that as long as a *memory-picture* of a person remains in the heads of relatives and friends, that person is alive as *mzimu*—a living-dead. On the basis of this perceptual evidence, i.e. the *memory-picture* (which can be reproduced in the brain of any human being), it is perfectly rational to assume that spirits exist. Westerners and so-called educated people have forgotten what an extraordinary experience it is to have the capacity to reproduce mentally, more or less at will, complete images of reality. Personally, I find great comfort in this ability to reproduce in my head lively images of my dear dead father and other close relatives. It is time to realize and acknowledge that belief in spirits is not absurdity or cultural atrophy but rational behaviour by intelligent people. The logic in the concept of the spirit, the *mzimu*, is: when the last person having a mental image of my father is dead, then my father is no longer a spirit—a living-dead—but has joined the ranks of the finally dead. On this basis, it is both rational and meaningful that people are in almost daily communication with the spirits of their relatives and ancestors. It is significant that the threat or the support that the village people feel they need in decision-making is perceived as coming not from the finally dead, but from the living-dead, the spirits.

EIDETIC IMAGES

The rationality of the concept of the spirit is supported by the sensory psychological phenomenon identified as eidetic images. Some people have the propensity to experience mental images so intensely that they actually project the image in space in front of their eyes. In my observation, this ability appears prevalent among village people who do not have a written language but depend on a strong visual memory for survival. Verification of this contention is problematic. Objects and animals may have spirits. As the spirit of a man is like the man, so the spirit of the tree or the lion reflects the physical form of each. As bodies and objects are divisible, so are their spirits divisible. Hence, if a girl wants a boy to like her, she puts a tiny piece of her nail in his favourite dish to be sure that his sympathy extends beyond the cooking vessel. When somebody says 'I have seen a spirit' it means 'I have seen a mental image.' It is as simple as that.

WORK IS A SPIRITUAL FUNCTION

Birth—life—sex—death. In this cycle of the living, the living-dead and the dead, every event and every function becomes a spiritual function. Forging the iron, ploughing the soil and herding the cattle are not only actions for survival, but also actions of communication and practical consultation with the spirits and God. Marriage, sex, pregnancy, birth, childcare, initiation are acts of spiritual communion which require proper preparation. Even the smallest menial household chores, such as collecting firewood, pounding maize or brewing beer from millet, assume an air of ritual. A family is not defined as the parents and the children. It includes the living and the dead and, above all, the elders and the spirits. It is the elders, with their knowledge of the proper preparations and correct procedures, who play a central role in the execution of many social, ritual and pragmatic functions. In the context of the shrines, the elders communicate with the spirits and receive their advice and instructions.

MEETING AT THE SHRINE

The shrine is the meeting place where the living and the living-dead come together. In my own life, when I have faced a difficult situation and not known which decision to make, I have found relief by imagining what my dead father might have done in a similar situation. Is there anything irrational in a behaviour which attempts to utilize such a source of information in a systematic manner?

An *mzimu* has no body. Sometimes, therefore, the relatives of a man may build a small hut where his spirit can settle and receive offerings and prayers. Others may use a rock, a cave, a tree or an abandoned house for the purpose. Various offerings, pieces of cloth, beads, maizemeal, small change and other things are made at the shrine to propitiate the spirits. Usually, it is the elders who perform this task. To grow old is to move closer to the spirits, receiving their advice and instructions, and thereby having control of this knowledge and its subsequent processing to other members of the community.

SPIRITS ARE MEMBERS OF THE FAMILY

As the family includes the spirits and the family's living quarters include the shrines, the question of village resettlement is complicated. Government planners and officials have made many unnecessary mistakes in connection with resettlement projects. Loyalty to the spirits of the family has been treated as superficial superstition, whereas it actually constitutes a rational, admirable and moving trait of character.

The elders have other important social functions aside from a privileged relationship with the spirits. In a family with many children, where one is usually being breastfed, the time of weaning is particularly stressful for the mother. As a result, it is a widespread custom in Bantu Africa and in many other cultures to transfer the child to the grandparents' home. This may be for a year or two or, in some cases, may even extend to the time of initiation or marriage. Usually, the child returns when he/she is able to pasture the goats or carry out simple household chores for the mother. Such a custom gives the elders a privileged and significant relationship with the children in the role of educators.

TRIBAL CULTURE AND ETIQUETTE

All societies have 'culture' in the broadest sense and in the most specific sense. This applies to people whose economies are based on subsistence farming, herding or hunting and gathering. Although etiquette may vary culturally, it is as important to a Maasai as it is to a western socialite. From a very early age, village children are taught correct, elaborate tribal etiquette. This includes the manner of addressing grandparents, father, mother and relatives with appropriate names, clan names or honorary terms. They must learn to memorize the seemingly inexhaustible list of ancestors, to express sympathy in certain terms when someone is coughing, sneezing or has been hurt, to receive visitors with appropriate greetings, and, generally, to behave according to the rules.

Of particular interest is the language teaching. On several occasions, among the Lozis of Barotseland in Zambia, I observed how meticulously the children were corrected in their use or pronunciation of words. Eloquence is considered an asset as valuable as money or food. There are also appropriate ways of handling or receiving an object from an elder. One is to hold the object in the outstretched right hand with the left hand clasped around the wrist (presumably this demonstrates that no hand is free to hit). I once observed Mukahamubwatu furiously rebuking a youngster who had offered Mukahamubwatu's pipe to her nonchalantly with the left hand. We should note, however, that the elders' regimen of formality is occasionally disrupted by the smiling and tender concessions universally bestowed by grandparents on their grandchildren.

TABLE MANNERS

The staple diet of the Bembas of Zambia is *nzima*, a thick maize mash eaten with a cooked relish of beans, leaves or—too seldom—fish or meat. *Nzima* is rolled in the hand to make an egg-shaped lump the size of a mouthful; the thumb is pressed into the lump giving it a deep dent; the lump is scooped through the relish pot in an attempt to collect as many tit-bits as possible and then eaten with great expectation! It is a display of bad manners for a child to make a dent in the *nzima* in the presence of adults and particularly in the presence of male elders. It is an expression of greed.

THE PROMINENCE OF THE ELDERS

The prominent role of the elders is not exclusively for the survival of the tribal tradition or for the benefit of the younger generation. Prominence also elicits the response necessary to ensure the survival of the elders and to make old age easier and more comfortable. Travelling the roads of Afri-ca, one observes small messengers scurrying off with a neat bundle in raised arms in front of them, the enamel bowl in a clean cloth, the share of the family food amply reserved for the elders. In a subsistence economy, the flock of children and grandchildren represent the future social insur-ance and welfare institution for the elders. In many ways it is a more deve-loped and humane system than that practised in western societies with their public store houses for the elders. In the extended family, the insti-tution of taboos tends to reinforce the privilege of the elders.

TABOOS AND BEHAVIOUR CONTROL

Taboos are prohibitions aimed at controlling certain types of behaviour. They exist in a multitude of forms, seemingly disconnected but in reality constituting a network of constraints which produce certain attitudes be-tween the different age groups. Most taboos are concerned with the con-sumption of food or the division of labour and are expressed in proverbial form. When an animal is slaughtered, it is divided according to strict rules decided by the elders.

One proverb says 'Teethless people must have soft meat'[30], another says 'A child who eats a fowl will fly away.' The thick end of a sugar cane (the sweetest part) is tabooed to children or their mothers will become barren. A pregnant woman must not eat eggs, lest she will have a child which will be bald as an adult. Boys must not eat the heart of a sheep, for it would make them cowards. Preservation of the division of labour is also secured. If boys cook food, they will fail to marry. If boys warm themselves by the cooking-fire, they will bleed excessively when circumcized, etc. From these examples, it is evident that the taboos are used by the elders to sustain their privilege. That does not mean that the enforcement of the taboos is always rigorous. With the children it is sometimes lax, but they must have earned the favour!

We should be cautious of reacting too fast in condemning such a device for social control. From the point of view of the survival of the whole so-ciety, the elders may deserve the titbits of their meagre privilege. The over-all social fabric promotes strong solidarity. In addition, there are devices which ensure that the superiority of the elders is not applied arbitrarily. If a youngster does not perform adequately according to the tribal standard, the parents and grandparents are blamed for not having trained him properly. Such a social rebuke is a humiliation. The Maasai say it this way: *Meirag te entim olotoishe* — He who has children cannot sleep in the bush.

MAGIC AND RATIONALITY

The concepts of the spirit and the taboo are devices for social control which operate to maintain the 'structure of authority' of a given society. This domain of mankind's conceptualization and activities is termed magic. Academically, the most popular way of treating the phenomenon of magic is to dichotomize and project it into a logical universe of rationality—irrationality. In such a language-trap, magic is irrevocably classified as irrational. And progress in this western sense becomes, by definition, impossible. It is necessary to observe and investigate magic in a disinterested and unbiased manner, asking not what magic is or is not but, more relevantly: How do people behave when they execute magical actions, subject themselves to such actions or object to such actions?

BLACK AND WHITE MAGIC

Initially, it may be useful to make a distinction between black and white magic, although this distinction is problematic and perhaps contentious. Black magic or black arts are executed by wizards, sorcerers or magicians of male or female gender. Generally, black magic is considered evil or malicious by the community. White magic is the purifying and healing magic. The equivalent terms in Swahili are *uchawi* and *uganga* respectively. Whereas an *mchawi* (wizard) is feared by the community and often diligently persecuted when discovered, an *mganga* (medicine man, healer) is allowed by the community, practises with the community's sanction, and is by and large appreciated. *Mganga* is the name of the man; *uganga* is his art. The origin of the verb *ganga* denotes all sorts of positive action from splicing and mending, bandaging and healing to saving from difficulty and setting free from charm. The lore also distinguishes another sort of medicine man, called diviner—*mwaguzi*. A diviner interprets dreams and omens, tells fortunes and prophesies events. He is a specialist in performing rites to remove spells and in curing illnesses caused by spirits. Often, he is asked to diagnose an illness. In practice, a man or a woman may be accorded all these abilities or only some. The important thing for us is to investigate the types of behaviour which are characterized as magic.

MEDICINE AS A CONCEPT

In the above context, the word *medicine* deserves special attention. *Medicine* is equivalent to *uganga* in Swahili, but the English word has been taken into daily use in many African and other languages. As a consequence, it has developed several meanings. *Medicine* is the oil which the white man pours in his car engine. It is the injection in the arm or the pill. It is the batteries inserted in the transistor radio. It is the fertilizer in the field. And it is, of course, the concoction or the powder prepared by the herbalist, or the amulet or fetish consecrated by the *mganga*.

In classifying magic and magic behaviour, there seem to be three crude distinctions which may prove useful. The first is that the spirits of the ancestors are important counterparts in a process of communication, i.e. consultation and worship. The second is that spirits of both living and dead can cause trouble, largely by their ability to enter into animals or objects to carry out evil work. The third is that men consecrated to magic can control the spirits of animals and objects and use them as medicine. It is important to understand the magic principle that the spirit of an object, i e the mental image of the object, the object itself and the name of the object form a unity, but a unity which at the same time is divisible. If an object is cut into three pieces, the spirit is still in each of the three pieces!

THE EVIL SPELL

Closely related to the notion of animal spirits and objects as medicine is the notion of the spell, *uchawi.* A spell is mostly evil. How to cast or how to remove a spell is a professional secret among the magicians, but lesser talents in the community are also having a crack at it as a means of intimidation.

Suzana Mutali in Lutonde village in Bembaland, Zambia, told me, while shivering with fear, that she expected to be mauled by a lion because my driver had cast a spell on her. He had a bracelet of braided lion hair which he had taken off and held up like a magnifying glass. Then he looked at her through it whilst mumbling a spell. Mukahamubwatu told me of a way she could harm an enemy. She would take a twig of a certain tree (she would not say which) and break it several times with loud cracks, mentioning the enemy's name, cursing him and repeating for each crack: 'Let his bones become brittle and break like this twig!' To bury a fetish, for example a crocodile claw, in the path or under a doorstep where an enemy is expected to pass is quite a common way of casting a spell. These days, one also meets more degenerate forms of magic. I once attended a healing session by a diviner at his hospital in the bush outside Lusaka. He took a battered telephone from a suitcase, threw the cord over the branch of a tree and dialled the spirits for a diagnosis and for advice on how to remove the spell on a patient who was standing in front of him.

MAGIC CONTROL OF REALITY

We should, however, not be caught by the conspicuous aspects of magical events, but rather try to understand the underlying thinking. It may appear that magic, once its conceptual premise is understood, is simply a rational attempt by people to control their reality. The first thing to be aware of is the tremendous value, impact and significance of the spoken word in societies which have a purely oral tradition. In the western world we have become careless with our speech habits because the written reference can always be resorted to. This is not so in the village.

THE VALUE OF THE WORD

Once the word is spoken, it is as binding as a written contract. A man with oratorical skills is admired greatly and, if his voice is also commanding, he is likely to make a career in the community. Village litigation is often won by clever wording and apt application of proverbial knowledge. Similarly, a curse pronounced in anger against someone may have the most serious repercussions for the offender. Once an oath is taken, the truth is likely to become known; once the village chief has voiced a decision or an order, people may grumble, but they are likely to obey.

In a climate of general reverence for and confidence in the spoken word, we may understand the fear engendered by the power of the word which carries a deep psychological impact. The casting of a spell or the magic incantation of a healer or sorcerer is met with the same plain belief in its practical consequences as the pronouncements of the elders on the prospects of the harvest or the orders of the chief regarding the village water supply.

... AND THE POWER OF THE THOUGHT

We who are from the so-called enlightened cultures, who belong to the age of reason, should pause for a moment and ask ourselves some questions. How is it that we have come to believe that our outer reality is insulated from the power of the word? In the world of magic, there is no distinction between the inner—logical—space and the outer space. It is quite natural to believe that one's thoughts, like one's hands, one's tools and other forces one controls, leave traces of effects on the objects and events in reality. We can see with our eyes that light reaches the objects and pervades the universe. The magician believes his thoughts do the same and perhaps we should not be too quick in insisting that his belief is wrong. What is happening in the process? When I think of this special table in my room, my desk, I do not suppose that my thoughts go through space and embrace it as the light from a torch. Rather, I have the notion that my thoughts deal with my mental image of the desk, namely *the concept of the desk*. But the question is: Why should it be more rational to think that my thoughts are dealing with *the concept of the desk* and not the desk itself?[31] We must realize that the thought-world of magic has no inner imaginary space. The dichotomy between form and content does not exist. Hence it may not locate thought dealing with real objects anywhere else than in real space and, conversely, the real objects in space cannot be insulated from the effects of thought. Although capable of it, the magician does not objectify in the sense discussed in the preceding chapter.

When the rainmaker wants to evoke rain or the medicine man wants to save a maize crop from pests, their thoughts, through the words of their incantations, are spreading themselves and contacting the physical objects of reality with their power. If it is a good thought or a good word, the maize plant will prosper from it. If it is an evil thought or an evil word, the plant will suffer. On its own premises, the magic viewpoint seems to represent a very sensible and consistent thought-universe.

INTENSITY AND REPETITION

Once the power of the thought and the word is accepted and the effect of that power on the real objects is recognized, it is an inescapable conclusion that the *intensity* of the thought is a decisive factor in controlling reality. In other words, the more intense a thought is, or the more intensely a word is pronounced, the greater effect it is likely to produce on and among the objects in reality. This is why notions such as *hope, will* and *desire* play such an obvious part in magical behaviour. Intuitively, we perceive that these words have something to do with *intensity of feeling* and, confronted with the adversities of life, few of us have escaped the idea that if we desire something strongly enough, it will materialize.

Remembering that the concept of the future is constrained to the notion of *an event afterwards*, we may understand that the ability to control this event is conceived as an ability to accumulate thought-intensity by a series of actions of *hoping, willing* or *desiring*. Hence the truly incessant repetitions which characterize most magical actions as well as dance and poetry in many societies. An invocation poem from the Igbo in Nigeria illustrates the point:

> Hills, take kola-nut
> Earth, take kola-nut
> Sun, take kola-nut
> Valleys, take kola-nut
> Ancestors, take kola-nut
> Go before us.
> Stand behind us.
>
> We don't eat kola-nut with its radicle*
> We eat what is due to humans
> We don't eat what is due to Spirits
> Take, all of you, your kola radicle
> Take, all of you, the slices of kola-nut
> Amen. Amen.[32]

* This expresses a food taboo. The radicle is reserved for the spirits and deities.

AN ORDERLY UNIVERSE

The rainmaker repeats his incantations for hours on end, the *mchawi* casts or removes his evil spells by repeating his secret formulas. In this world of spirits and ancestors, of *willing* and *desiring*, it is only natural that everything happens as the result of will. I can, at will, invoke the presence of my father's spirit, i.e. my mental image of him. The magic universe is an orderly universe in which every object and every event has its special place and its special cause. In many Bantu languages, it is not possible to express exactly the western notion of a *coincidence* or a *happening by chance*. In such a thought-world, it is also consistent to devote much attention to the notion that the detail is decisive for the whole. Mukahamubwatu insisted that a concoction of the roots of the *Mukula* tree would cure a person from intestinal worms—but the concoction, which was a soup, would lose its healing power if it was stirred with the right instead of the left hand.

OBSESSION WITH DETAILS

The medicine man is commonly given a chicken as part payment for a treatment, but if the chicken is not caught at sunset the treatment will fail. The rainmaker's incantations are interrupted by a black bird flying up and he must begin again. Because the rites often fail to have effect, the attention to detail develops into obsession with detail. If a desired effect fails to appear, it is naturally assumed there was something wrong in the process of preparation. The magic world is an excessively orderly, structured and, consequently, predictable world for its inhabitants. Because events continuously take place outside people's control, it is also a world in which miracles and wonders are daily, normal and natural happenings. Although gods and spirits may be unruly and give people a life of complexity, the purpose of gods and spirits is, nevertheless, to create greater simplicity in the complexity.

DRUMMING AS REGULARITY

As I write these lines, the drumming in the neighbouring village has been going on for hours. In Bembaland, the bass-drum, called *kayanda*, carries the rhythm steadfastly. The drummer virtually hits your muscles with his hands. The smaller drums are called *mongfuza*, which means something akin to *chatterbox*—and they sound like it. The drummer pulls your nerve strings with his fingertips.

The role of rhythm, regularity or repetition in our perception of the world, was elaborated on in the previous chapter. We showed that sensory motor processes taking place simultaneously or in short sequence are perceptually organized in the same *whole*, so that one process has a tendency to produce the other—or the expectation of it. In our quest for reduction of uncertainty, for processing information about reality, we encode and store information by utilizing what can be traced of regularity.

I O I I O I O I I O I O I I O I O I I O I O I I O

In perceptual terms, there is no difference between this series of visual impressions and the acoustical impressions of the drum vibrations in my ears and muscles. In both cases, it is an incessant rhythmic repetition of certain sensory impressions. This is why, with some justification, we can ask if any essential difference exists between scientific behaviour and magic behaviour? Why this dichotomy between science and magic? Are we confronted with another language-trap? Both attempt to control social or physical transformations in reality. What does science do that magic does not?

REPEATING THE REPETITIVE

Science searches for the repetitive in order to establish predictability of events, i.e. to acquire information and the subsequent feeling of certainty. The methodology of magic is similar to science in its search for and understanding of the secrets of the repetitive, but it fails in establishing predictability of events. Magic establishes the feeling of certainty merely by repeating the repetitive.

In magic invocations and incantations, in tales, legends and myths, in the poetry, in the pictorial and decorative arts, in the architecture and handicraft of traditional societies, there is this persistent quest for the certainty of information through a repetition of the repetitive. It is as if reduction of uncertainty is achieved through the repetitive images which permeate the culture.

MAGIC SCIENCE AND SCIENTIFIC MAGIC

The use of magic, however, should not lead us to believe that all behaviour in traditional societies is conditioned by it. People are very pragmatic and rational in their intercourse with the spirits. There are many clear scientific traits in magic behaviour as there are many magic traits in the behaviour of modern scientists. Diagnosis and treatment by a medicine man of a person who is sick due to a spell is a combination of practical psychological insight and magic imagery. The modern sociologist does not fare much better with his incessant quantification of magic models and fashionable theories, the results of which change as fast as the scale of observation. Neither science nor magic can be judged by its cases of degeneration. Magic may lend itself to the exploiter, so does science.

A DANCE-POEM

The re-creation or reconstruction of the repetitive patterns in reality is illustrated in these stanzas from an Igbo dance poem called *Igodo*.

— — —

Blow the musical horn
Odo by Nkwo market inspires you
Fourheaded Odo inspires you
Odo by Ngwu tree inspires you
Blow the musical horn

Let our Earth take 'qwhq'
Take 'qwhq' and pray
Let our Hills take 'qwhq'
Take 'qwhq' and pray

A Hill is never a valley
Take 'qwhq' and pray
'Qwhq' is our weapon

One holding on to 'qwhq' is never lost
One holding on to 'qwhq' possesses truth
One holding on to 'qwhq' lacks nothing
Sun is watching
Heaven and Earth are watching

— — —

It is Odo who is saying it
Almight Odo is saying it
Sons of Almight Odo
We are celebrating Igodo
We are singing Igodo
We are drumming Igodo
We are dancing Igodo

Cock has crowed (about 4.30a.m.)
Bush fowl has chanted
He who visits has to depart.[33]

— — —

The dance-song goes on until the early morning. Participants seem by their insistent, continuing effort of repetition here and now to try to accumulate effect on the future, the event afterwards.

IMITATIVE COMMUNICATION

In our example

$$I O I \ I O I O I \ I O I O I \ I O \ I O I O I \ I O \ I O I \ I O$$

we may perceive this series of signs or configurations at different levels of complexity. We may say that it is 'a kind of ornament' or a 'linear scroll-work' consisting of the signs I and O put together in a certain manner. Or we may say that it is a necklace stretched out on a table consisting of sticks and rings in the pattern IOIIO. With a little more imagination we might suggest that the signs represent a visual interpretation of a series of drum beats in which the sign I represents the beat, the sign O represents the pause, and the sequence of signs illustrates the rhythm of the drum beating.

In the last two examples, we may say that the signs *imitate* events or objects in reality. They are imitative *interpretations* of objects or events in reality. If we had known the *context* from which the series of signs had been taken, i.e. a woman who is stringing necklaces or a musician with a drum, we might identify the above two instances as examples of *imitative* communication.

Some people prefer the word *analogic*.[34] The word imitative is more accurate, however, because it implies the action of communicating by imitation. The essence of imitative communication is that the message is coded in a form of magnitudes and in relationships of magnitudes which correspond to the magnitudes and relationships in reality. It is this circumstance that makes the picture of a smiling face look like a smiling face. Simply expressed, imitative communication is pictorial although not always in a photographic sense. It is built on the idea of *likeness* between the message itself and the object or event in reality which the message represents.

DIGITAL COMMUNICATION

It may be useful to realize that our example can be perceived on yet another level of complexity.

$$I O I \ I O I O I \ I O I O I \ I O I O I \ I O \ I O I \ I O$$

This series of signs is also a series of binary representations (IOIIO) of the decimal figure 22. In the decimal code we are accustomed to use, there are ten different symbols, 0 to 9 inclusive, and we repeat them in a multitude of combinations to express magnitudes. With the advent of the electronic computer, organized on the principle impulse/no-impulse or current/no-current, it was necessary to apply a language which uses only two symbols, i.e. O and I. These are called a binary system and communication based on this principle of impulse/no-impulse is conveniently called *digital* communication. It does not serve our purpose to provide an in-depth explanation of the binary computer code, but it is worth noting that a telephone number 22-14-09 translated into a digital code would read as follows: IOIIO-OIIIO-OIOOI. In contrast to imitative communication which is, in a sense, linked to reality through the perceptual phenomenon of likeness, digital communication and the interpretation of a digital message appears completely liberated from such a link. It objectifies its concepts in an *inner* space. Digital communication takes place by means of invented signs which are tossed around according to certain rules. Fundamentally, digital communication is a social convention, something which people have invented and modified over the years to suit very practical needs.

A WRITTEN LANGUAGE IS ESSENTIALLY DIGITAL

In an earlier chapter we traced the invention of the written language. The old pictographic languages, such as Egyptian hieroglyphs, represent attempts at imitative communication. Understanding of the written symbols was linked to the recognition of a likeness between certain symbols and certain objects or events in reality. In the course of their development, these languages required thousands of different signs, became unwieldy, and were discarded. When man discovered that he could link a sign with a certain sound in his mouth, that he could put the signs together in words and sentences utilizing only a very small group of signs, the alphabet, he emerged into that epoch of digital communication which has culminated with the electronic computer. The understanding of a phonogrammic written language is liberated from this requirement of likeness between symbols and objects or events in reality. Such a language is abstracted from reality. It is in a sense a reality of its own. Much linguistic and semantic research remains to be done, but there is little doubt that our written languages are essentially, although not totally, digital in nature. In mathematics and the science of logic, the digital character is clearly visible. The negation with the word *not* serves as the best example of the structure of digital language. 'Either he is coming today or he is not coming.' 'If this is an apple, everything else is not an apple.' Verbal language, however, is not quite so purely digital as written language. In conversation between two people, one can easily observe components which represent imitative communication such as certain modulations of voice when talking about certains events, facial expressions, pauses, gestures, etc., which provide the context of the spoken words and cannot be isolated from them.

CROSS-CULTURAL COMMUNICATION

This detour in the field of communication should bring us closer to an explanation of the concept of the spirit and the wizard, the process of magic thinking and the magic world-view in general. Whereas magic thinking maintains the *one-ness* of the world, digital thinking creates the *two-ness*. The magic world is a world in which there are no objects, because all objects are events. It serves no purpose to make value judgements about whether one mode of communication is better, more desirable or more rational than the other. We are now in a position to identify and define more clearly the nature of the cross-cultural communication process, particularly if we think of it as a process between the modern western and the traditional Third World society. (There may of course be other kinds of cross-cultural communication processes which we do not consider here.) *Fundamentally, cross-cultural communication is a process which has to build a bridge between imitative and digital modes of communication.* This problem is the focus and objective throughout the rest of this book. In the opinion of many experts, the human brain is partly imitative (analogic) and partly digital in its operation.[35] Of interest is the fact that scientists are now capable of building not only digital but also analogic computers.

CAUSAL RELATIONSHIP THROUGH LIKENESS

The magic world view is a world with a concept of 'causal relationships' based on the principle of *likeness* and simultaneity. The magic universe is one in which thoughts, things and events are identical when they are like each other. The thought of a thing is identical with the thing itself. The thought of an event can cause a similar event to happen. Simultaneity or closeness in time between two events is the factor which establishes the notion of a 'causal relationship' between them. 'A pregnant woman should not eat fish. If she does, her foetus will slip out.' 'If you walk on Mr A's farmland, he will cast a spell on you by *picking up* your footprints.' Classification of objects and events are made, consequently, on appearance and practical applicability rather than on abstract criteria. Mango and banana *belong to each other* not because they are both fruits, but because they are both edible. The magic way of thinking is alive in all societies, in daily life as well as in institutions of higher learning. Least of all should we assume that magic thinking has an uneven geographical distribution, limited to the populations of Third World countries. The magic thought-world is a rigid universe in which each event and object is assigned a place, thereby becoming predictable. It is one of mankind's heroic attempts to reduce the uncertainty of human existence.

INFORMATION RESOURCES CONTROLLED BY THE ELDERS

This chapter began by pointing to the status of Bantu elders in their societies. Countless proverbs testify to the prominent role they occupy. This prominence also applies to the elders of other societies in the world, strongly based on an oral tradition. The Kikuyu say: *Hari muthuri hatii-tangagwo mai*—In the presence of elderly people one must not pour water, i.e. nobody is allowed to be foul-mouthed when elderly people are present. Or *Ikinya ria mukuru rikinyaga muruna*—Old people's walking teaches young ones to walk. Or *Kahiga gakuru gatiararagwo ni maai*—The stream does not pass over an old stone, i.e. through respect for its age. Or *Mukuru, gaya, unyonie mugaire*—Old man, divide, and teach me how to share. This shows how the Kikuyu respected old people, whose responsibility was the distribution of meat, beer, etc. at all gatherings.

The Maasai say it in another way: *Emunyak irorei loo lootoishote*—The words of the elders are blessed. In Swahili there are still other ways: *Asiyesikia la mkuu huona makuu*—He who does not listen to his elder's advice comes to grief. Or *Penye wazee haliharibiki neno*—Where there are old people, nothing goes wrong.

The prominent—and dominant—role of the elders is obvious. Analysing such proverbs more critically, we discover that they are concerned with the knowledge of the elders as a resource fundamental to the survival of the society. The behavioural code and practical experience accumulated by the tribe through the process of trial and error over the centuries is vested in the elders.

THE NONSENSE OF ANIMISM

Foreigners have failed to sense the profoundly spiritual character of the world views of the African peoples. What is labeled animism and ridiculed as a kind of superficial idolatry, is in fact religious insight of great human maturity. It represents a compassion for the beings and objects of this world from which western civilizations should take a lesson.

Of course there are spirits. It is, however, a misunderstanding to infer that the spiritual expresses itself in the physical, when the world is perceived as singularily spiritual. In this universe of spirituality the magic of the word is omnipresent.

John Mbiti[12] quotes a hymn from the Pygmies about the nature of God. For a novice it expresses the religious experience no less succinctly than the Bible:

> In the beginning was God,
> To day is God,
> Tomorrow will be God,
> Who can make an image of God?
> He has no body.
> He is as a word which comes out of your mouth.
> That word! It is no more,
> It is past, and still it lives,
> So is God.

MEMORY AND INFORMATION STORAGE

In other words, we can regard an oral society as a system for the processing of information in which the brains of the elders are the main units for the storage and retrieval of relevant information. Bearing in mind that there is no written language in which information can be stored, we can appreciate the overwhelming importance of a good memory. For an observer, the great capacity for remembering complex detail displayed by village people without a written code is a striking impression.

Why is it so desirable to become an *mzee*? Certainly, there are the social benefits of old age, good and free food, the privilege of getting drunk—but there is also the more serious side. To grow old is to grow closer to the spirits. The spirits are included in the social system of the living. The family is an unbroken continuity of spirits, elders, parents and children, each category with interrelated rights and duties, hence life after death must be perceived as complete as life before it. The elders are the gatekeepers in people's continuous process of communication with the spirits. It would be wrong to say that the elders are accorded supernatural powers, because all powers in a traditional society are, in a sense, natural and the miracle of survival is a daily happening. This explains why the notion of wisdom and reverence of old age is so closely connected with that of witchcraft. A wizard or a witch could never be a youngster. It takes a lifetime to acquire the truly complex secrets of the profession. This does not exclude the earthbound pragmatism of the people which is evidenced in the Swahili expression *Mganga najigangi*—A witchdoctor does not cure himself.

BELIEF IN WITCHCRAFT EVERYWHERE

Is witchcraft a phenomenon today? Here is an excerpt from the sports page in today's newspaper under the headline Warning on Witchcraft: 'Concerned at the mounting plight of witchcraft in football, the African Football Confederation has launched a war against the practices in an effort to stamp it out. At a recent meeting of the CAF executive held in Lagos, Nigeria, it was resolved to ask the Confederation's secretary, Mr Mourad Fahmy, to send out a circular to all the national soccer bodies of the member countries drawing their attention to the practices of witchcraft and superstitions which have become a common phenomenon in soccer . . . For many years, teams have spent a lot of money to hire the services of witchdoctors to put spells on their opponents and help them win matches.'

The political field is equally exposed. Recently, a candidate who failed to be returned to parliament filed a plaint at the National High Court. He alleged that the winner of the election committed acts of witchcraft during the campaign meeting to influence people to vote for him. The specific magical acts of wearing a roll of star-grass round his right ankle, pointing at the crowd with a medicine horn, and spitting and cursing at the plaintiff's chair were given as examples. The plaintiff claimed that, as the result of this, people left the campaign meeting out of fear and the presiding officer left the polling station unattended, thus rendering it vulnerable to malpractices.

The reader should bear in mind that this is not very different from the advertisements for aphrodisiacs or the column on horoscopes found in almost any western newspaper. And when a famous person brings another to court in a libel suit for a defamatory statement, he probably does so because he believes in the *spell* of the word. The word has an effect, it is as simple as that.

Talk to the old men, discuss their ideas, wrestle with their wits, win them via their own cunning . . .

. . . but listen to the old women.

8
the oral civilizations

> '. . . And the old man spoke to the child:
> ''I have brought you to this place that you
> might view the mountain of God, that you
> might know the home of your father's
> father. And it is here where I shall tell you
> all the ways of the people of Maa, that you
> may never forget them whatever comes to
> pass in your life. Do you hear, my child?''
>   And the child answered: ''My father, I
> hear''.'
>
>   From Wisdom of Maasai, I.O. Sidai

THE ABILITY TO LISTEN

When a Westerner arrives in the office he says 'Good morning' and re-
tires in sullen silence behind his desk, reading his mail or possibly the
newspaper. When a Swahili speaker arrives he says 'Habari gani?' i.e.
'What is your news?' and he expects to engage in a conversation about
yours and his news. The Somali herdsman is even more graceful. Imagine
your weary arrival at his camp where he greets you with, 'So maal', i.e.
'Go and milk my beast'. I believe that the greetings in a culture are a gate-
way to an understanding of that culture.

A couple of years ago, I shared accommodation with Yaba Walaga at
Vudal Agricultural Station, Papua New Guinea. He was a very competent
bushman from Yagusa Valley in Eastern Highlands Province. We spent
many evenings talking together about bushlore: how to trap wild pigs and
birds, how to track people, and how to read the signs of the forest. One evening, Yaba Walaga suddenly stopped talking and said, 'I can hear David
Drayeu is coming.' I could hear only the chirruping of the grasshoppers
and said, 'No, its too late, David has gone to bed.' But Yaba Walaga insisted; he knelt down and placed his ear against the cement floor and said,
'I know David Drayeu is coming and he carries something heavy.' Soon
after, David Drayeu knocked at the door with a bag of sweet potatoes on
his back!

At the station we were a team of 20 to 30 people and Yaba Walaga was
able to identify many of them by their footsteps, as well as a multitude of
other sounds in the cacophony of the rain forest. This highly differentiating acoustic perception is an ability totally lost in western cultures. We
have also lost sight of the psychological value of the greeting and the so-

cial value of communication generally. Simple human conversation is a disappearing social phenomenon. Most oral information is now fed into electronic devices or written on machines. Most of what we hear and see emanates from the same type of technological media.

OUR VISUAL CONSPICUITY

The western cultures (or should we say the western mono-culture?) are focused on the visually conspicuous, the moving images, and the monumental material manifestations. We have arrived at a stage where we conceive the present as the apex of human achievement. We conceive the world as a world of skyscrapers, staggering bridge spans, giant dams, moonflights and supertankers. Our tourist industry glorifies similar experiences from the past: the Acropolis, the Colosseum, the Eiffel Tower, the Pyramids, the Sophia Mosque, Venice. For the aesthete, there exist the visual and tactile revelations of a Picasso, a Moore, a Cellini or a Michelangelo. Little by little, we have come to believe that civilization is synonymous with stone monuments or other material manifestations.

CULTURES OF SOUND SYMBOLS

Because of our emphasis on material culture, we have not been responsive to the fact that the evolution of mankind has also fostered great oral civilizations. These cultures do not express themselves to the same extent in stone or other physical materials; their cultural testimony lies in the transient sound symbols of musical instruments or the human voice. These civilizations have mastered the transience of their means of expression in a truly miraculous way. Most of them have survived thousands of years of environmental hazards—much longer than any western culture—against the odds of a long history of colonial domination. The oral civilizations are still alive in Africa, Latin America and Asia and their manifestations are no less monumental than those of the material cultures.

PROVERBS AND STORIES

In anthropology, the emphasis on description and analysis of the material objects of a culture is quite understandable. These objects represent accessible, tangible, unchanging manifestations of a culture which can be classified, measured and interpreted. However, oral monuments also exist and are available to the ready listener and observer, despite language problems. The forms that oral civilizations have used for survival are structurally simple, functionally efficient and often display a spectrum of aesthetic qualities from the humorous to the poetic. Oral culture is preserved in the form of proverbs, riddles, songs and stories. In addition, there are myths, legends, tales, epic poems and ballads. There is considerable variation in the form and expression of all these above, which are usually accompanied by dance and music.

A single proverb or a single folk tale is not very sensational. Quite understandably the average foreigner may encounter an oral civilization without realizing the value and implications of its oral tradition.

The definition for our investigation of oral culture forms is the following: culture is how people structure their experience conceptually so that it can be transmitted as knowledge (information) from person to person and from generation to generation.[36] This definition links language to lifestyle and looks generally at culture as a system for information processing.

LANGUAGE AS A MODE OF ACTION

To understand the function of the proverbs or the stories, we need to consider language as a mode of action rather than an expression of thought. The narrative language is not analytical; it aims to re-create the event and therefore derives from the event itself. The hunt provides a good example of an event. Some years ago I participated in a net hunt in Isoka district, Zambia. This form of hunt requires cooperation and the formation of different groups with different functions. The women and the youngsters act as beaters while the men stretch the nets and stand guard with bows or spears in strategically placed clusters. Sometimes a bush fire is started to drive the animals in the desired direction. When the hunt is in operation, it is a revealing demonstration of concerted social effort and pointed verbal interaction. It becomes apparent to the observer that an individual participating in the hunt does not perceive himself or herself as an individual, but as a functional part of the communal operation, a community member in an inextricable sense.

That same evening, around the village fire, the hunting event was replicated literally. The actions were imitated in gestures and sometimes dance steps; the driving, coordinating force of the words was accentuated. The event became a story. I was left with the feeling that oral language was born through the emergency of action in a hunting event. The story plays a sustaining role in the maintenance of social formations. Perhaps the event was also the origin of social formations.

There is another quality or function of the story. People around the fire with their backs to a wall of darkness: their words flow to create bonds of solidarity, to reinforce the feeling of certainty inside the fragile light of the community circle. The story plays a sustaining role in the maintenance of social formations.

ARE YOU READY TO LISTEN?

In most Bantu languages there is a standard phrase with which the storyteller begins: 'Are you ready to listen?' The listeners respond 'Yes, we are ready.' Judging from the listeners' attentive reactions, the eloquence and sophistication of the storyteller are highly appreciated. His talents are not limited to the fireside chat. Village litigation, village ceremonies, and the recent institution of the roadside bar provide forums for the expression of his talent. Village people, particularly the elders, have a meticulous sense of what constitutes proper tribal language, and take great pride in children who speak correctly at an early age. Foreigners possess grossly distorted ideas about the verbal capacity of villagers and schoolchildren.

PERFORMANCE IN A SECONDARY LANGUAGE

People who are profoundly knowledgeable and articulate in their mother-tongue are judged by foreigners on their verbal performance in a secondary language, such as English. And in most Third World countries, English has often been taught either inadequately or insufficiently. From personal experience, I know that it is seldom realized how limited the vocabulary of a second language speaker is. If the foreign English teacher in an African secondary school has a vocabulary of 40,000 to 50,000 words, the students probably acquire 10 per cent of that by the time they leave school. Access to their thinking and the scope of students' abilities is hardly possible given this linguistic restriction, yet foreigners make judgements on this basis. Considering that the students come from and still belong to oral civilizations placing a high value on the capacity for verbal articulation, the injustice of these judgements is ironic.

FROM STORY TO LEGEND

What is a good story? In Swahili the word *kisa* denotes both story and event (*mkasa*). Whatever the origin of the story, it probably developed rapidly into a means of expression for the storyteller personally, as well as for his knowledge. Ultimately, the story became the 'story with a moral', summarizing and expressing the life experience of generations of tribal members. More generations passed and the stories became the tales of the elders, the revered pronouncements of tribal wisdom, and when the stories became the pre-history of the tribe, the tales became legends. The storytellers, the old men and women, were professional in their craft. The tales and the legends became the common spiritual heritage of many tribes. While retaining the main structure and point of the story, each storyteller contributed his verbal embellishments. Above all, the art of storytelling was to link the story to a current event or conflict in the village, so that its moral might make a graphic impact on the listeners. The children, of course, were often the primary target for the storyteller. The stories were the means for educating children in socially approved behaviour and conduct. The moral content of the stories espoused the success of virtuous qualities, the defeat of vice, the virtue of mercy, cunning, humility or courage, and revealed the folly of laziness, rebelliousness or snobbery. Storytelling is still vibrantly alive today. This can be observed by anybody staying in a village over a period of time. It is worth noting that storytelling seems to develop in the listener the ability to 'illustrate' the story in his mind as it proceeds. It is my impression that people in oral societies have very visual memories. They easily construct 'mental maps' and demonstrate an ability to follow practical procedures on the basis of verbal instruction only. Unfortunately, the importance of recording oral literature is not yet fully recognized. To illustrate the special insight and educational content of the stories, three of them are reproduced here.

THE STORY OF THE LION

Once upon a time a small lion cub wanted to hunt with his older friends, but his father said, 'You are too young, you will be hurt during the hunt or get lost in the high grass. I think you should stay at home.'

The cub begged his father, 'Please father, let me go hunting, I am old enough for that.'

After a while, the father felt sorry for the cub and said, 'All right, you may go, but keep in company with your friends or you will get hurt.'

Walking out in the world, the cub stopped often and looked at everything and soon fell behind his comrades. Suddenly he was alone and did not know where to go. He was lost. He became frightened. Remembering his father's warning he started running. He came to a place where many elephants were eating. Suddenly a large elephant stepped on the little cub and killed it.

The other lions soon realized the little cub was missing and they started looking for him. They were very worried and before long they found his body.

'This is terrible' they agreed, and went home to tell the father.

'Your son is dead' they said to the father.

The old lion began to cry. 'Who killed my son? Who?' he shouted. Then he roared, 'I will punish the killer!'

The other lions told him, 'The elephants have killed your son. He got lost at their eating place and a large elephant stepped on him.'

The old lion stood quiet, thinking for a while, then he suddenly said 'The elephants did not kill my son. The goats killed him!'

'No sir, that is not so,' the other lions cried to no avail. The old lion roared, 'Don't interrupt me! I know the goats did it! The goats did this terrible thing to me!' And off he stalked in fury.

When the lion located a herd of goats, he killed many of them as a punishment.

Very often when a man is hurt by someone powerful, he punishes someone who is weaker than himself.

In terms of life experience, this story is a treasure chest with a double bottom. For the youngsters it demonstrates the folly of thoughtlessness and it provides a very astute observation of adult psychology.

THE STORY OF THE MILLIPEDE

The millipede child was learning to walk. One day it stood looking at all its legs and said in despair, 'Mother, I have so many legs, which one should I move first?' The mother looked at her child and answered mildly, 'Move, my child, move.'

THE STORY OF THE FATHER AND HIS THREE SONS

Once an old father who wanted to test his three sons said, 'Here is one shilling for each of you; go to the market and buy something to fill my room.'

The oldest boy thought this was an easy task. He went to the market and bought straw.

The second son, who also thought it was easy, went and bought feathers.

The youngest boy sat down and thought for a long time and said to himself, 'What can it be that costs only one shilling and fills a room? What is it my father wants?' He thought very hard. Then he went to the market and bought a candle and a match.

The father rewarded the youngest son. When the light filled his room, he was so pleased that he gave the youngest son all his land and cattle.

RIDDLES AS EDUCATIONAL DEVICES

The riddle is another educational device which the elders use to communicate knowledge or exert control. The use of riddles is also surrounded by a sense of the ceremonial. Although the elders take pleasure in dispensing this challenging type of wisdom, they have to be cajoled into it and the setting must be right.

It took Mukahamubwatu a great deal of spitting and several pinches of tobacco before she finally condescended to ask riddles—and then only after sunset. In Swahili the narrator begins the ceremony with the expression *Kitendawili*—Here is the riddle—and the listeners reply *Tega*—Set it. If the listeners fail to solve the riddle, the narrator will say *Nipe mji*—Give me a town. The listeners will then name a town they would like to visit, such as Mecca, and the narrator will tell a story about his imaginary journey to that town.[37] The narrator will revel in all the good things which the journey enables him to enjoy and mock the listeners who have failed to solve the riddle. Cunningly, he builds up his listeners' expectations before he bombastically reveals the answer to the riddle. It is interesting that the listeners resent naming a town which provides the narrator with an opportunity to enjoy his fictitious travel. In the Kenyan town of Lamu, a major Swahili seaport, people used to organize riddle contests during important celebrations. The contestants were, in turn, placed in one of the high-backed intarsia-decorated 'Lamu chairs' to emphasize the social significance of the contest.

EXAMPLES OF RIDDLES

Here are some examples of Swahili riddles presented in their English translation:

My house is small but it has many windows. *Answer:* A fish-trap.

My ladle cannot get into my water jar. *Answer:* Bottle.

A tree has fallen far away, but the branches have reached here. *Answer:* News of a death.

He goes on for ever, but never reaches his destination. *Answer:* The sun.

I came across a long chain on the road, but I could not pick it up. *Answer:* Safari ants (which walk in a row).

The black slaves are hanging from a tree. *Answer:* Eggplant (which has long black fruit).

When I beat my child, people dance. *Answer:* The drummer.

My house has a well-thatched roof, but when it rains it leaks everywhere. *Answer:* The mango tree.

The lady's veil is waving. *Answer:* A flame.

I always hear him, but I cannot see him. *Answer:* The wind.

RIDDLES AND EUPHEMISMS

Whereas the educational value of riddles may not always be overt, an observer cannot fail to recognize their importance for the overall system of information processing in oral civilizations. Information is power and the elders control the information resources of the tribal community. The riddle has the unique feature of yielding power to the person who knows the answer, thus enhancing his social image. At the same time, it exposes to slight ridicule those who cannot find the solution. Through this technique, the elders can sometimes play a very subtle game.

The riddle may also have another function. It may function as a mechanism for euphemism. In many oral civilizations, certain things or people are not referred to by their actual name, but circumvented via synonyms and metaphors. This derives from the notion that there is no difference between the name of the thing and the thing itself. Therefore, even mentioning the name of a thing or an event might inflict harm or ill fortune. The chief is not mentioned by his name but called, for example, 'the snail of the rain', meaning he is as gentle as a snail and his coming is as unexpected as that of the rain.[38]

Such circumlocutions are quite common in all tribal languages. In English, for example, we are inclined to use the expression 'He went to sleep' — when we mean he died. In Amharic, circumlocutions have been developed into a conversational art called 'wax and gold', referring to the wax mould and the gold cast in it as the reverse of each other.

VILLAGE LITIGATION

The Amharas in Ethiopia hold in high esteem the orator who can phrase his remarks with such subtlety that when he says one thing he actually means the opposite. For example, in village litigation an accused flattered to extreme is being insulted. Generally, in oral civilizations oblique references in speech are perceived as cleverness and inspire respect. Conversely, a blunt and direct speaker is considered to lack finesse. He does not allow his listeners the opportunity to demonstrate their 'intelligence' through their own interpretation of what he says.

The children are the most obvious recipients of the grandparental (or most often the grandmaternal) wisdom in puns and riddles. At an early age they are taught to appreciate metaphor and allusion and to understand when they are being subjected to subtle insult. To know one's audience, to be a good judge of character, and to understand what is really being said are considered signs of social intelligence, a highly developed quality in traditional communities. The speaker and the listener are not behaving verbally in the abstract, they are continuously watching each other's behaviour. The truth value of a statement is verified or falsified in the context of comparing behavioural expression, stance and conduct.

THE PROVERBS OF TRIBAL WISDOM

Proverbs which predominate in oral civilizations represent the essence of tribal wisdom and knowledge. They are always presented in a semantically pointed form and are sometimes phonetically euphonious. Whereas stories are often told by the women to children, the 'saying of proverbs' is usually the prerogative of male elders.

Through proverbs, Mukahamubwatu commented continuously on life in general and on life in the village in particular. It was not a question of using a proverb now and again, every tenth sentence was a proverb. This mannerism was not unique to her but fairly common among all the elders in the village. Proverbs are a common feature in most traditional communities, but foreigners have not described them often or valued them seriously. In part, this may be due to language barriers.

The use of proverbs is truly extensive and it should not be doubted that they exert a 'magical' influence on people's minds. Proverbs should be examined in the behavioural context in which they are spoken. Above all, proverbs are the instruments through which the younger generation are instructed to become viable social members of the community.

AS THE PROVERB SAYS

As an Ethiopian proverb says, 'The person who grew up without correction will find his mouth slipping instead of his foot.' Note my expression 'As an Ethiopian proverb says'. This is precisely the phrase the elders use when they relate a practical situation to a proverb. The behaviour of the young, actions taken by the adults, happenings in the environment—in short, the daily events of the village—are continuously evaluated by the elders. Quite simply, it is information processing by analogy. Actual events are scanned, then accepted or rejected in a process of comparison with proverbial knowledge about similar events.

Bana Enifa's old mother in Luwingu complained to her daughter that all her children had left for the Copperbelt and she seldom heard from them. Bana Enifa said 'I am here in the village with you.' The old lady answered, 'Like the proverbs says, one stone will not support a cooking pot.' (This proverb is a reference to the traditional hearth which has three stones to support an iron cooking pot—and, indeed, less would not do).

'As—or like—the proverb says'—this comparison is expressed in the Swahili word for proverb *mithali* (or *methali*), which simultaneously means a likeness, a resemblance or a similitude. This concept explains something to us about the function of the proverb in the oral society.

PROVERBS COME FROM THE SPIRITS

Proverbs are not considered to be man-made, they come from the spirits and the ancestors. We must appreciate that a proverb uttered by an elder on an appropriate occasion is not just a verbal frill; it comes to the listener as an awesome revelation of the wisdom of the spirits and its truth is irrevocable and undisputed.

A Chaga tribesman from the slopes of Kilimanjaro recalls his first confrontation with the truth of the proverb:

I well remember the first time I was told a proverb I was about 15 years old and had to accompany my parents to the plain to hoe. The day was exceedingly hot and I began to grow limp. I wished I could return to the mountain with those lucky people who had finished their work early. My father said, 'Let us rest a while.' But when we started to work again I almost fainted. My father scolded and threatened that he would beat me if I gave in. My face became sullen, my heart was full of bitterness and I gave up chatting with my parents. When we rested again, my father, seeing my face, called me to his side and said, 'My child, he who suffers tribulation will in the end enjoy rest.' 'This' he continued, 'is a proverb of our elders which teaches us a lot. By the time you eat the maize we are planting now you will remember and understand.' [39]

PROVERBS AND BEHAVIOUR CODE

That proverbs function as mechanisms for socialization and control of group behaviour is illustrated by the following examples from various African languages. Only the English translations are provided.

Amharic:
When spiders' webs unite, they can tie up a lion.
He who knows much, does not speak much.
Don't catch a leopard by the tail, but if you do, don't let go.
Thorns prick lightly the man who walks slowly.

Kikuyu:
The property of a helpless man must not be divided before his death.
The buying of a wife begins from a little thing (i.e. great events have small beginnings).
The piece of cloth in another's bag does not patch your own garment.
A market can be spoilt by one woman.

Maasai:
The neck cannot rise above the head (i.e. a son should not disobey his father).
The chip in the fire laughs at the one in the woodpile (i.e. a fool never sees his own foolishness).
A zebra does not despise its own stripes (i.e. one should not abuse one's traditions).
Only the weak cow knows how to care for itself.
A house does not fall while its main pole is standing.

FOLK HUMOUR IN PROVERBS

Although proverbs demonstrate the use of observed detail which succinctly incorporates a moral lesson, they often execute this through humour as these translations from Swahili testify:

For a fly to die on an ulcer is not bad (i.e. he got what he wanted).
A fight between grasshoppers is a joy to crows.
A cow is not oppressed by its own hump.
The gratitude shown by a donkey is a fart.
He who is naked squats low.
Everyone who stretches a skin on a drum pulls the skin to his own side.
Love is like a cough, it cannot be hidden.
A hungry man observes no taboos.

BEHAVIOUR CONTROL—PRACTICAL ADVICE

With the last proverbs we return to consider the taboo. Taboos are occasionally expressed in the form of proverbs. Together with so-called 'beliefs' and 'superstitions' they constitute a body of knowledge usually based on some empirical or practical foundation. It would be more accurate to call taboos 'assumptions of casual relationships'. The control of behaviour seems to be their primary purpose. Here are some Swahili examples:

If a man goes to bed without washing his feet they will be licked by the devil.
Looking at a naked grown-up person will bring blindness.
If you give someone with hiccups a big fright, the hiccups will go away immediately.
Don't drink water from a ladle without shaking it hard first.

The purpose of the last taboo is to ensure that the water is clean and free from insects. There is nothing particularly 'superstitious' about such practical advice. It is important to watch out for the tendency in western societies to characterize other cultures in terms which have an image of scientific observation but in fact lack an empirical basis. Over the years, the oral civilizations have been subjected to many unjust misconceptions under the guise of objectivity.

REVERENCE FOR THE WORD

In comparison with oral civilizations, we lack the reverence for and sincerity in the treatment of words which is a prevalent characteristic of oral cultures. We no longer understand that once a word is said it has an irrevocable and fatal consequence, because it has been said. In oral cultures, the potential effect of a derogatory word is particularly awesome. The earthbound Maasai have a proverb which demonstrates this precisely: *Menyanyuk enchicati enkutuk o eno siadi*—i.e. The odour of the mouth (words) is stronger than the odour from the anus.

THE ETIQUETTE OF PROVERBS

A social etiquette prescribes the application of proverbs. Young children are often taught or entertained with tales and stories which are a little less solemn than proverbs. A youngster must reach a certain age before being addressed in proverbs by the elders, i.e. before the essence of tribal wisdom will be revealed to him. The youngster must know the etiquette of using proverbs. It is, for example, disrespectful for an adolescent to quote proverbs in front of the elders. He or she must learn when and how to use them. It takes a considerable period of time to memorize hundreds of proverbs, a sustained observation to discover their application in social situations, and frequent practice to master their application successfully. In oral civilizations, eloquence and proverbial knowledge are prerequisites for social success. Age is another prerequisite, while control of the main food resource, be it land or cattle, is an ultimate prerequisite. The Maasai are attributed with acknowledging two resources, cattle and proverbs, and these are held in almost equally high esteem.

THE ORAL LANGUAGE IS SUNG AND DANCED

The odour of the mouth is stronger . . . People born and bred in a written culture cannot perceive the intensity of the word of mouth. In the oral civilization, the word comes from a behavioural context. The oral language is sung and danced and drummed. It comes from sweating bodies in work or play. It has a tactile quality which can be touched and smelt. It activates all the senses of those who participate in the process of communication. This is not so in a written culture.

THE WRITTEN LANGUAGE IS REDUCED TO THE SENSE OF SIGHT

The reality of a book is that our perceptions are reduced to a single sense of sight while sitting in a chair. It is a stunning fact that a mere 100 years ago, in industrialized countries, words were still largely spoken by people to people. Now, as words are spoken more often by, to and through machines, the result is that people are, quite literally, less and less in touch with each other. The word has lost its tactile quality because we do not learn as much from observation and experience; we learn from books.

THE PARADOX OF WRITING ABOUT TALKING

Sitting here writing, I am in the paradoxical situation of being forced to describe a fundamentally oral phenomenon in a medium which is completely alien to it, namely writing. My reader is confronted with the fact that my description of the oral civilizations cannot be 'real'—it results from the analytic process that writing itself entails.

My description exists only in the writing. Through the invention of the written language, the abstraction, the negation and the logical universe, we lost the 'one-ness' of the oral civilization for the sake of the descriptive 'two-ness'. We had to invent the concept of eternity to escape the godforsaken dichotomy of our 'scientific' thought processes.

The written language is fundamentally an internalized language. It reduces our perception of the outer reality to the sense of internal sight. Nobody can dispute the merits of the written language in all its forms from literature to mathematics, but it also separates people by putting itself between them. We are paying a price for the miracle of the digit.

ENCODING OF INFORMATION IN PROVERBS

I said earlier that basically science looks for the repetitive and tries to trace regularity in order to cope with the enormous amount of sensory information confronting us in any given situation. In that connection, we discussed the phenomena of encoding and decoding,

IOI IOIOI IOIOI IO IOI IO IOI IO

which are methods to rationalize the process of storing the above series of digits in our memory. This is achieved by the regular recurrence of IOIIO, which can then be given the form 'IOIIO by five'. This is a matter of thought-economy. We can now recognize that the oral civilization, like the written, is a social formation which has developed its own mechanisms for processing information. In terms of function, there is not a fundamental difference between the oral proverb, the written word or, ultimately, the digit. The proverb is a language mechanism for encoding information by observed regularity in the empirical data of the respective society.

For clarification, let us again resort to a proverb: *Enya enkalaoni nkishu*—An ant may eat cattle.

Surely, after slaughtering sick animals or passing carcasses in the bush these herdsmen have, over periods of time, regularly observed tiny ants consume a cow in a matter of hours. With equal regularity, they have observed in human society how a 'small', unimportant person can sponge off and destroy a man's wealth. The essence of the proverbs is its parable between two or more social or natural phenomena which resemble each other and occur with some regularity: *Mithali!*

The information is coded in a very thought-economical way in the constellation of the concept of the ant (insignificant in size but powerful) and the cow, which for the Maasai is synonymous with wealth (relatively enormous in size but vulnerable). In the pointed form of the proverb, the information is easy to code and memorize and equally easy to decode and retrieve when required. The proverb is like a phonetically punched card or an oral computer chip, for the processing of information.

PROGRAMME FOR PROCESSING OF INFORMATION

The story, the tale, the legend, the myth, the ballad, the epic poem or the riddle—although none may have a form as pointed as the proverb—we should now see how together they constitute a functional programme for the processing of information which is unique to oral civilizations. There are tens of thousands of proverbs and stories vibrantly alive in today's tribal languages. We are confronted with a human creation of monumental dimension and grace—the disappearance of which would be a tragic loss in the annals of our heritage. That the marble of the Acropolis has survived for thousands of years is a marvellous testimony to human accomplishment. That an architecture in transient sound signals has survived the same timespan or longer is a more unique achievement, which requires modern technology for its preservation.

THE TRIBAL ELDERS AGAIN

In a type of social formation such as the tribal society, it is the memory of the elders which functions as the unit of information storage. Consequently, it is also the elders who control the storage and retrieval of the information resources of the society. These information resources involve an enormous amount of descriptive detail, which is successfully mastered by members of a respective village through unique techniques for coding and decoding. Our definition of an information programme was simple. It is a description of reality which an individual or a social formation uses for information processing and with which it acts in accordance. This is the tribal law. Consequently, any attempt to direct social transformation and behavioural change has to address itself first to the issue of transforming the fundamental programme for information processing. Traditional societies do undergo change. What is characteristic is that their pace of transformation is slower than in industrialized countries. Why is this so? The answer lies in an investigation of how this type of social formation maintains and perpetuates its programme for information processing.

Childhood is probably a culturally conditioned concept. We cannot be certain that all children have a childhood. It should be the right of a child to be a child, to explore, create and master the environment. Social transformation inevitably begins with the child.

Gladys is an elder who is not that old, 48 years only. She is treated with the utmost respect by her five daughters and one son. She takes particular care in communicating tribal values to her grandchildren.

It is important for all persons involved in this tense village litigation meeting in Shoa, Ethiopia, to follow etiquette. Social conventions are often a great convenience in minimizing conflict.

The village council works its way towards a consensus, sometimes slowly, but it works!

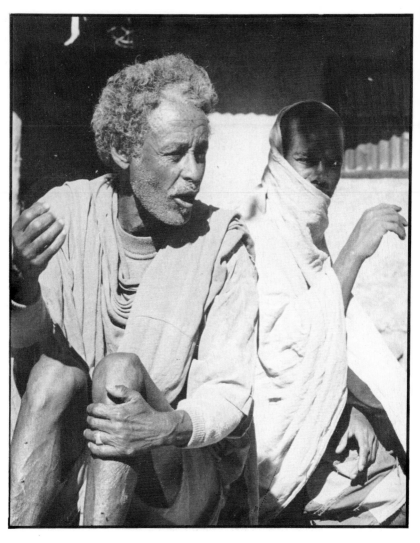

To twist a phrase in a striking way and turn it into a proverb gives the speaker a reputation for acumen and leadership.

Taciturn eloquence sits on the mountain slopes of Tigre, Ethiopia.

9
under the mango tree

> ' No system of education can be analysed
> or criticized apart from the society which
> it is designed to serve. Education and
> society are interdependent; it is society
> which sets the goals which education
> follows. The society itself must first be
> understood if its goals are to be fully ap-
> preciated.'
>
> *J. P. Ocitti*

> Omunsi egi abantu begela ali banu
> bainunulana—*Most achievements come
> about by imitation.*
>
> *Bahaya proverb, Tanzania*

EDUCATIONAL SYSTEM IN THE VILLAGE

The school or the adult literacy class in the shade of the village tree, often
a tree with an abundance of mangoes, is a familiar picture to the traveller
in Africa's rural areas. This tableau is a fairly recent phenomenon, which
has not yet made a significant impression on rural society. The village has
its own educational system or, shall we say, system for the processing of information. This system is created in response to the particular needs of a
rural society and it meets these needs in a functional and efficient way.
Statements implying that people in or from rural societies are uneducated
are deeply embarrassing. These statements, which do not take into consideration indigenous educational systems, are expressions of ethnocentric
prejudice. Firstly, it should be recognized that learning does not take
place only in learning institutions. Secondly, it should be acknowledged
that efficient learning institutions are not necessarily or exclusively those
modelled on the western educational system. In the preceding chapter, we
investigated that aspect of the village educational system which is concerned with the content and form of educational instruction. The ' curricula' of oral civilizations are the proverbs and the stories. We also investigated the role of the teachers, i.e. the elders. In this chapter, we shall endeavour to describe the learning process as it is organized and/or institu-
tionalized in the village society.

CHILDREN HAVE A SOCIAL ROLE

Once I stayed in a small village about 90 kilometres from Choma in

Tongaland, Zambia. I happened to sit with a group of children in the evening and I asked them, 'So, what are you going to do tomorrow?' A small boy answered, 'I shall herd the goats.' A bigger boy said proudly, 'I shall herd my father's cattle.' A girl said, 'I shall work with my mother cleaning maize in the storehouse.' Another girl said, 'I shall make baskets to sell at the market.' Then there was a little boy who did not say anything, who just stood looking down, making scrollwork in the sand with his big toe. I said, 'And you? What are you going to do tomorrow?' He looked at me with an uncertain and slightly embarrassed smile and said, 'I shall go to school.'

What was important to the children was their certainty about the social value of the role they played in the family and the community. The little schoolboy did not feel he had such a role.

LEARNING STYLES

The children's perception of their role was obviously related to the learning style practised in the village and the fact that it was radically different from the style in the western-inspired schoolroom. Broadly, we can categorize three dominant types of learning styles: learning by observation, learning by peer group and learning by instruction. It is the last type which quickly lends itself to institutionalization. The first two learning styles still play a dominant role in rural society. Learning is not concept based; rather, it is an extra linguistic process. Clearing the bush for a *chitemene* garden, threshing with the oxen, riding the camel and preparing millet for beer brewing are not learned from situations specifically designed to transfer information orally to the child, but through the process of observation and participation.

THE CHILD AS A 'LITTLE ADULT'

The child learns from direct interaction with the objects and the tools of the adult community by following as a 'little adult', literally in the footsteps of the working mother or father. On several occasions, I have observed a little girl or boy take a tool and imitate the movements and gestures of the adult, be it weeding the maizefield or carrying a water bucket. From that moment on, an informal apprenticeship between the child and the adult is established. The adult may walk more slowly and occasionally give assistance or correction, but I have rarely observed oral explanation or instruction take place. Clearly, in subsistence economies where food production is seldom high enough, imitative learning is necessitated because all hands are needed for survival, including the very small ones. The ultimate purpose of this learning style is a level of performance equal to traditional performance. There is a requirement for imitation and perhaps not so often a felt need for innovation.

THE WESTERN LEARNING MACHINE

We are mistaken if we think that imitation is a sufficient explanation of how learning takes place in a village society. What it may explain is the lack of motivation sometimes felt by the village child when confronted with the western learning machine. The concept-based teaching of written culture is a meaningless hurdle which the child can sometimes tackle only by imitating the conspicuous features of the teaching situation. Hence the endless repetition of jingles with accentuated pronunciation and intonation by the teacher, but without the meaning, or the meticulous copying of sentences from the blackboard into the notebook, again without the meaning. With ingenuity, the child adjusts to the classroom situation by adapting the learning style of practical observation used in the village. There is no such thing as students without motivation; there are only students accustomed to different learning styles.

'PROPER TEACHING'

Once I taught nutrition to a primary school class in Zambia. I discovered that the students were not really interested in seeing a slide series, because it was not proper teaching. Proper teaching meant I should write sentences on the blackboard which the students could copy in their notebooks. Only then had I, quite literally, given them some pieces of my knowledge. The early Bible teaching of the missionaries probably reinforced this particular learning style.

GRANDMOTHER'S HOME—A LEARNING INSTITUTION

Previously, we mentioned the transfer of the child to the grandparental home as one typical pattern which may occur in the course of a child's development. Often, this is the place where children are taught tribal etiquette and given practical knowledge through proverbs, stories and other oral forms. This arrangement can be characterized as an educational institution, i.e. a social formation with the purpose of processing information.

INSTITUTIONAL PREPARATION FOR INITIATION

The educational activities which take place prior to the initiation or circumcision of girls and boys have a profound significance. These activities are basically common to all tribal cultures, although they differ in form, content and duration. In some societies, the youngsters undergo tuition by the elders or the magicians for months. In other societies, the preparation for initiation continues for years. Often the teaching period for initiation purposes is so thoroughly organized that it is quite justified to refer to an educational system of initiation schools.

CIRCUMCISION, A LEARNING EXPERIENCE

Foreigners are under the impression that circumcision as a social practice is fading away, but this is not entirely so. The Maasai of Kenya still practise circumcision and have an extensive and well-organized educational system supporting its continuance. Young Maasai boys spend their early years herding their father's cattle. At the age of 13 they leave their families to gather in special *manyattas* (camps). Manyattas are schools for young warriors where they are taught bushlore, defence of livestock and people, strategy and tactics in lion hunting, and skills of war, as well as songs, dances and tribal traditions. The educational period may last up to eight years. At a certain point during this education, the *morans* (young warriors) return to their homes and the actual operation of circumcision is carried out and celebrated. Similar educational institutions exist among the closely related tribes of the Samburu in Kenya and the Boran and the Galla of Ethiopia. These nomadic pastoralists trek thousands of miles in search of grazing and water for their herds—often through very hostile environments. To survive such hardship requires an intimate and extensive knowledge of people and nature. Far from being uneducated, these people possess a system of knowledge comprising such subjects as veterinary sciences, social psychology, meteorology, ecology, zoology, geography and herbal medicine. Anyone who has observed pastoralists in their milieu can testify to their great skill.

A DISGRACE TO BE UNCIRCUMCISED

Although data are not easily accessible or reliable as to the number of African tribes which practise circumcision, we know that many do. More important to our discussion is the fact that circumcision is accompanied by a process of transmitting information to the initiates. It should be noted that an initiation ceremony is, above all, a social event of the utmost significance. It does not necessarily include the act of being physically circumcised. In countries where Islam predominates, the social significance of initiation is particularly evident.

It is interesting that the Swahili word for uninitiated and uneducated is the same: *siofundishwa*. The medical implications of the circumcision of men or women are not germane to our discussion; rather, we emphasize its social importance. For a boy to be called *siofundishwa* is a profound disgrace. Circumcision is a test of manhood and a sign that the circumcised has gained full adult status. Considerable social pressure builds up around the issue. Boys are teased that they will not be able to stand the pain and the ceremony is usually imbued with secrecy. If a boy behaves disgracefully under duress, he can expect to be ridiculed. There is a deliberate accumulation of tension which is released after the event, usually by lavish celebrations, congratulations from relatives and words of admiration and comfort from proud parents.

We can look at circumcision in several perspectives. It can be interpreted as a power game enhancing the position of the elders who control the ceremony. On the other hand, for people always on the edge of survival in an environment requiring the utmost in hardiness and endurance, circumcision is an educational test of critical importance. Pain is a minor adversity in life; through self-discipline and courage people learn to survive. The tribal experience may well be that those who are uncircumcised succumb in the fight for survival. From a legal and social perspective, circumcision qualifies decisions concerning marriage, inheritance, and other social and economic transactions.

EXAMINATIONS IN BUSHLORE AND TRIBAL LAW

Circumcision is usually also associated with other initiation ceremonies, such as magic ordeals, which may now be disappearing. The Chaga tribe, farming on the slopes of Kilimanjaro in Tanzania, used to send their boys to initiation camps which terminated with systematic examinations in bushlore, agriculture and tribal behaviour.[40] Lessons were given by the elders in the form of didactic songs. Examination was through the use of riddles and, significantly, the novice's powers of memorizing were tested. A lesson on protocol and home care might teach the correct way of going in and out of a door to avoid danger. In a bent position, a man must always raise his head to be on the alert for ambush. While approaching home, a man should whistle or sing, lest he surprise his wife in an act of adultery or find his mother or sister undressed. Proper care of a pregnant wife by her husband would also form part of the instruction. A husband should be amenable to practical observations necessary to maintain his wife's health as well as the ancestors' good will. For example, a husband should assist in carrying heavy loads and in placating the idiosyncrasies of his wife's emotions. This is antenatal care of considerable insight.

Detailed lessons on sex were also part of the curriculum of this educational institution. In order to avoid illegitimate offspring, a serious offence in tribal law, young men were advised to have intercourse with old and barren women.

A WOODEN TALLY AS A NOTEBOOK

The teachers frequently used textbooks or notebooks in their lessons in the form of tallies. These were wooden sticks on which the content and sequence of the lesson were indicated by carved symbols. The tally functioned as an aid to memorizing the enormous amount of detail communicated in complicated lessons. The simpler forms of lessons were talks to support and exemplify a specific proverb.

THE SONG SHAPES ACTION

Singing as a pedagogical method is held in great esteem. Song is, in a sence, intensified speech and as such is a more powerful incentive to action than a spoken word. Sometimes it has a magical aspect. The song, through its compelling rhythm, shapes mood, action and even the character of the student. The substance of the song has less impact.

A VILLAGE SCHOOL OF HOME ECONOMICS

Initiation of women is strictly segregated. It takes place in a similar school-like institution but the duration is usually shorter. It starts after the onset of menses and focuses on educating the young woman as sex partner, mother, housewife and farmer. For example, a lesson on virginity, an important ethic in tribal law because of its value for legitimate reproduction, would urge the following:

Be eager and open your ears like a trap, my children, for now you are circumcised and have been fattened to be beautiful of shape. Protect your virginity well. Do not yield to a youth who tempts you, but run away. Do not walk in the dark for you may be seized by force. Do not let a youth see your breasts or thighs for he may desire you. When you have preserved your virginity, your family will honour you on your wedding day with gifts and celebrations. Guard your virginity! If you do not, it is a disgrace for your family and all the people will spit at you.[41]

EDUCATION BY OTHER EVENTS

In the rural village, central events, aside from initiation, function as educational institutions. They vary from marriage or funeral ceremonies to the celebration of a good harvest or the inauguration of the shrine of an ancestral spirit. Common to these events are the complex rites expressing tribal wisdom to the participants and spectators as well as control by the village elders.

HEREDITARY PROFESSIONS

Finally, we should recognize that regular oral instruction does take place in teacher/student situations. This applies in particular to hereditary professions such as magic and herbalism. These professions involve thousands of concepts impossible to communicate without detailed oral instruction and demonstration. This type of instruction is not widespread. The herbalist, as an example, is not likely to entrust his professional secrets to anyone but his eldest son. Moreover, the herbalist will transmit his professional wisdom only in his old age. Occupational training is provided by people skilled in the crafts of pottery, blacksmithing, woodcarving and carpentry. Although not universal, these educational activities are such regular features of village life that they can be considered institutions.

THE INDIVIDUALISTIC INDIVIDUAL AS A WESTERN INVENTION

Society sets the goals which its educational institutions follow. Each society develops the educational system it needs and *all* societies have educational institutions and educated people. The general objective of every educational institution is to process information from one generation to the next. The particular or specialized goals of institutions may vary. In western society, the process of socialization sanctifies the individual as a separate member of society, socialization becomes a process of individualization. In traditional societies, the process of socialization emphasizes a person as an integral part of a social system, a community member, because this is essential to the survival of the group. In traditional societies, an individualistic person is perceived as an oddball—if not a wizard. Freedom of the individual is clearly subordinate to the interests of the village and the tribe. We cannot fully appreciate this until we realize that 'the individual' is a concept invented in western society. All human beings do not necessarily feel they are individuals. Moreover, there is no universal, rational reason why they should feel so.

SENSING THE VILLAGE CONSENSUS

You may well ask what the western society has lost on the way to its present state of democracy/technocracy. In a village in Papua New Guinea, people have a leader called Karikara Kiva Haela, i.e. he who takes care of the village. When he says, 'Today is a fine day for fishing,' the people prepare for a day of fishing only if the leader has interpreted correctly the conditions for the action and the community's moods, if there is a consensus.

Leadership is an active, subtle process of interaction. If a leader makes a wrong judgement, he is not followed; if he repeatedly fails in his judgement, he is no longer the leader. This is leadership exclusively by the quality of its performance in a communal action. During a discussion on the proceedings of a meeting on appropriate technology, Aron Kunja from East Sepik Province, PNG, expressed the attitude of consensus succinctly: 'I do not like to have a chairman. I am from the village where everybody talk and they are old enough to know to talk the same thing. We are not talking the same thing here.'

COMMUNAL ACTION

There are many examples of the nature of socialization and communal action in village life. The Acholi tribe of Uganda practised a system of cooperative farming under the leadership of Rwot Kweri, a hard-working person with organizational talent and an ability to interpret and voice the communal mood.[42] The farming area, plotted long in advance, was quite large. Controlled burning was the technique used to clear the ground for cultivation and reduce subsequent weeding. Labour-intensive crops such as finger-millet and sorghum mixed with lentils and beans were cultivated. Digging, planting, weeding and harvesting could only be carried out through a system of strong cooperation among the families and members of each village. Land was communally owned and worked. The village, the clan or the tribe could only survive through communal effort.

These social goals and needs lead to the development of the educational institutions found in the traditional village societies.

If western civilizations have offered science and technology to the progress of mankind, the oral civilizations of Africa and other continents have offered an equal achievement in their profound knowledge of human and social relations. But that knowledge has been scorned or ignored.

LEARNING FOR SURVIVAL

Traditional educational institutions in the village have taught and continue to teach people to survive effectively in their environment, often with great appreciation for the survival of the environment. Under changing conditions, this is breaking down. The knowledge is not adequate for the changing demands of the economy. Nevertheless, the efficacy of this education is conditioned by the static nature of the traditional society. These societies are in a process of very slow transformation, almost imperceptibly from one generation to another. This education is not a mechanism to introduce change; rather, it serves to maintain the *status quo*. In this system, students are highly motivated to learn since the knowledge is directly related to the prescribed role of each person and the application of the knowledge is essential to individual and group survival. The western educational model as it is practised in Third World countries does not cope in a relevant manner with the realities of students' daily lives, whether they are children or adults.

LACK OF EDUCATIONAL SYNTHESIS

The existence of indigenous educational institutions and learning styles has been ignored. Western educationists have been blind to the oldest and truest pedagogical rule: start with what the students *know*, not with what *you* know. They have failed to recognize the need for a synthesis between the educational traditions of the oral civilizations and the requirements of a modern concept-based learning method.

As mentioned earlier, the professional attitudes and value judgements made by educators should be regarded with suspicion. A grotesque superimposition of cultural values has taken place. It is not the privilege of the educators to list preconceived requirements in terms of knowledge and skills that define an educated adult. Most educational programmes in the Third World are culturally oppressive because they are conceived behind desks. All efforts for the enlightenment of the masses, whether via formal or non-formal educational systems, are essentially reflections of the power structure of the respective societies.

These educational efforts demonstrate the misconception that people are objects to be formed or cases of ignorance to be treated, not human minds whose ingenuity and creativity are the ultimate resource of any social transformation. We are far from recognizing that people realize themselves in social transformation and economic productivity not through better knowledge, but through more confidence. When people confront a situation where they need specific knowledge, they acquire it. If, at that moment, the education required is available, so much the better. Although educational efforts or government incentives are important, they cannot in themselves release the creative energies of the individual or the community in a process of directed social transformation. Fundamental trust can.

FROM ORAL TO WRITTEN CULTURE

Educators and so-called development experts have devoted much discussion and effort to the use of a foreign language as a form of colonial oppression. For example, English or French as the language of learning are used in secondary schools or adult education classes in Third World countries. It is argued that people preserve their cultural identity only through use of the tribal or national language. Clearly there is truth in such a consideration. However, the discussion has obscured the more fundamental issue of formal or non-formal education in the Third World, namely the directed transformation from a predominantly oral to a predominantly written culture. This is the issue: the transformation from an oral civilization in which the events of reality are predominantly classified in functional terms to a written culture in which the events are objectified and internalized in predominantly logical concept formations.

FROM IMITATIVE TO DIGITAL INFORMATION PROCESSING?

Ultimately, this transformation is the same as the transformation from a basically imitative (or analogic) to a basically digital programme for processing information about reality. There is, however, a clear indication that command of the technology of the written language is a prerequisite for the command of all other technologies derived from it. Therefore, it is necessary to ask some controversial questions. Is universal literacy a prerequisite for a desirable social transformation? If so, is it desirable to forgo the deep knowledge of social relations which the oral culture fosters? Or is it desirable or possible to find a *modus vivendi*?

INTEGRATION OF THE DISINTEGRATED

Along with its advantages, the written culture exhibits the potential for confusing our perceptions of what constitutes social transformation. Not reality itself, but the differentiating dynamics of our written language lead us to perceive social transformation as consisting of components such as agriculture, health, nutrition, education or technology. The dynamics are so influential that we even organize government ministries and international organizations according to similar professional definitions. It is no wonder that when confronted with this conceptual disintegration of reality, we feel the need to invent the concept of 'the integrated approach'. The written language is deceptive if we do not understand what we are doing with it and even more so than is the case with the oral language.

Because of the complexities involved in the processing of information in oral civilizations, it is untimely to draw or to attempt conclusions regarding formal and non-formal education, cross-cultural communication or media application for Third World countries. There is no easy recipe for making a radio programme or an educational film. The reader should make up his own mind. True to their oral nature, these phenomena should speak for themselves under the mango tree.

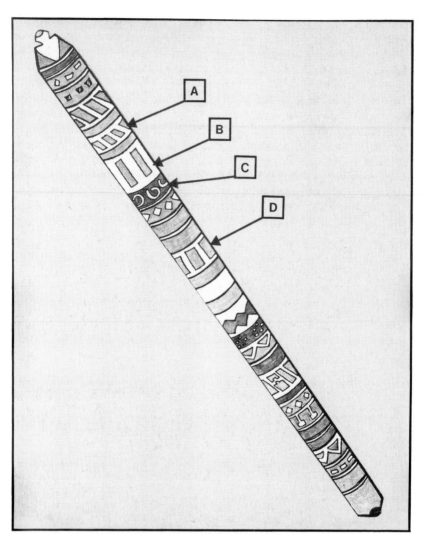

The decorative value of artifacts from tribal societies is attracting attention, but the practical function is little understood. This Chaga tally[43] is a device for the processing of information. It is a 'notebook' in analogic language, used by an elder when instructing initiation novices. The following are some of the points that the teacher wants to remember.

A. A woman's ribs are more bent than a man's because she has to support the embryo; therefore, do not despise her.

B. When your mother gave birth to you, she split open like that; therefore, do not despise her.

C. When you were in your mother's womb, this is what you looked like.

D. The female sex organs are like the railings separating the animal quarters from the centre of the hut. They are alike for all women. God made them.

Cimfuti is a student at Kamoto Primary School in Eastern Province, Zambia. School is far from home, so Cimfuti sleeps from Monday to Friday in a hut he has built behind the outhouse. He prepares his own meals from green leaves and maize flour. Learning to write and reckon is harder than herding the cattle, especially when you are hungry.

Sheraf el Nouhoud from El Obeid is ten years old. He does not go to school, but is educated by following in his father's footsteps—on a camel. Every evening he uses the camel to pull water from the well with a long rope. The well is 50 metres deep. A great deal of water is needed for 150 head of cattle.

Adult literacy class in Mali. Governments supported by agencies of the United Nations and other international organizations have implemented scores of educational programmes, often with little impact. Significant averages of the situation in African countries show that 70-90 per cent of the population cannot read or write.

Adult literacy class in Ethiopia. There are 10-20 per cent more people unable to read or write in rural areas than in urban areas. There are 20-30 per cent more people in the old age group who cannot read or write than among the young. The rate is consistently higher for women than for men.

The transistor radio could revolutionize adult education in Africa, but its potential has never been realized. Broadcasts in tribal languages are sporadic and inadequate in quality. The programming is alien to the people's oral tradition. These women from Chipata, belonging to the Nyanja-speaking Ngoni tribe, did not like the announcer because he did not speak 'proper Chinyanja'.

10
the method of no method

' *That this nation under God, shall have a
new birth of freedom; and that
government of the people, by the people,
and for the people, shall not perish from
the earth.*'

Abraham Lincoln

' *I don't make jokes; I just observe the
government and report the facts.*'

Mark Twain

' *Liberty is the mother, not the daughter
of order.*'

Pierre Joseph Proudhon

HUMOUR AND DESPOTISM

To work with people is easy because they have a sense of humour. The biggest obstacle in working with a government is that its very nature is against humour. Humour is the best indication of mental health and resourcefulness. It is a liberating mental mechanism from the constraints of authority, conventionality or morality. No government can afford to entertain a sense of humour about its policies and programmes. People survive or escape government by protest, strike, terrorism, revolution—or by laughing at it. Government of the people is acceptable, so is government by the people, but when it comes to government for the people, people start to laugh.

Western society is built on the idea that people elect representatives, thus delegating overall control of their lives to social formations such as governmental institutions. In return, these institutions create and promote the myth that society will disintegrate unless people obey the written and unwritten laws of the institutions. The extension of this myth may lead to the demand for law and order, the declaration of a dictatorship, or the ultimate rule by despotism.

BENIGN OPPRESSION

When the word govern was still pure, it meant guide. Karikara Kiva Haela does this in a village in Papua New Guinea. He succeeds in guiding the people of the village by his constant sensitivity to the direction in which they want to be guided. He guides by the notion of a 'sensed consensus'.

Nowadays, the word govern includes connotations such as authority or obedience. Underlying these concepts is the assumption of a power to punish. Government authority *rules* society. The majority of people do not manifest a need to question this rule, because often government is a benign form of oppression. Experiencing an intensive process of socialization which promulgates the necessity of government authority, many people do not realize that human society without government is both possible and feasible.

THE LAUGHTER OF THE DINKA

One of several tribes in Africa with a non-hierarchical social organization is the semi-nomadic Dinka. These pastoralists migrate annually between the wet and dry season, grazing their cattle in the Nile basin of South Sudan. A few years ago, I worked for a short period of time with a group of Dinka on a health education project in Khartoum. All the participants were medical assistants or sanitarians attending an in-service training course. They were characterized by a gentle and mild manner, equally given to bursts of work and bursts of fun and laughter. Particularly hilarious were the attempts by the government officials and medical authorities to 'lecture' them and 'structure the programme' of the course.

The spontaneity of the Dinka was not an act of irreverence. Rather, it was a Mark Twain kind of laughter, a laughter of lenience.

The Dinka, who comprise about one million people, do not have any central tribal authority, i.e. no hierarchical structure. The society operates through a cluster of social formations which coexist in a state of functional equilibrium. The formations are continuously changing the composition of the cluster by fusing with each other or subdividing. The precipitating factors in the process seem to be the varying demands of economic realities and the necessity to diffuse the build-up of human tensions occurring in any social formation where people work and live together for long periods of time.[44]

The Dinka place a high value on their independence, while appreciating their tribal unity. The Dinka sense of independence is not antithetical to their strong sense of cultural identity or to their sense of tribal loyalty. We have something to learn from listening to how people laugh.

AN 'UPRIGHT' DANCE

Although the Dinka may also be a serious and furious man, he wears laughter in his limbs. Like the Maasai, the Samburu or the Boran of Kenya, who are also cattle herders, the Dinka have upright and slender bodies which they move with profound grace. No authority, no tension in the neck, and a laughter enviably at ease in their muscles. Like other migratory pastoralists, the Dinka have little sympathy for he who stoops to till the soil. The attitude of uprightness expresses itself in their dance, which moves vertically rather than horizontally—a characteristic which seems to be common to all cattle herding tribes. It could be said that they jump in groups, but the word jump is too clumsy. Their bodies soar upwards in an undulating movement which presses a resounding breath in and out of their chests. It is a rhythmic movement which pulls in the spectator. In the dance, men compete to jump the highest, a valuable skill for a herdsman who must keep track of stray animals in savannah grass taller than himself.

ORDER WITHOUT AUTHORITY

Before sunset, in clouds of red Sahara dust, I saw hundreds of Dinka tribesmen dancing in groups on the outskirts of Omdurman. They appeared to behave not as individuals, but as a cluster of cells in a huge tribal body, a social formation optimally functional for group survival in a tough environment. The Dinka society survives by an order, but not the order of centralized authority. This human reality, despite its possibilities, remains unpracticed.

FREEDOM CONDITIONED BY BONDAGE

In western societies, the concept of the government and the concept of the individual are linked. There cannot be government without individuals. There cannot be supreme authority without individual responsibility. Power to punish, rule by law, passing of judgement are unthinkable without an individual's acceptance of guilt. Monotheism flourishes on an individual's admittance of sin followed by atonement. The concept of the freedom of the individual emerged as a reaction countering the coercive actions of governments; it is, therefore, inextricably linked to the existence of an oppressive authority. As long as an individual's thinking about freedom is conditioned by the concept of bondage, it will remain an unfree endeavour. The notion of the individual is a deception which ultimately favours the ruler(s) of individuals. The individualism so esteemed in western civilization is unknown in many others. In the history of western societies, there is an unbroken round of applause for the hero, from the Homeric saga to the popular cult of Superman. For the mass, there is only contemptuous silence. Yet we now know that the genetic basis for the creation of the exceptional individual is generated by chance in the mass itself.

Governments govern by educating individuals for the end purpose of being governed. To govern and to educate are, in practice, the same thing. The verb to educate literally implies a mechanical process in which quantities of information are transferred from a person who knows to a person who does not know. This process is an action exercised by the authority of knowledge.

THE COMMUNITY EDUCATES ITSELF

Any system or method of formal or non-formal education should be regarded cautiously and critically. And any educational method will have special implications in Third World countries. No educational method exists which is not an imposition. If there is a way, it should rather be the method of no method.

Social order can be imposed by terror or through the mechanism of atonement; it can be enforced by government bureaucrats and police officials. However, a functioning order without centralized authority is also possible. Decentralized mechanisms operating to maintain society are particularly apparent in many tribal societies with a marginal existence. Order without authority arises spontaneously. Quite simply, communities of human beings are capable of thinking and acting together in shaping their common destiny. This old truth is either largely unrecognized or repressed in western societies. Proudhon understood this when he said, 'Liberty is the mother, not the daughter of order.' The education of individuals does not bring about the social transformation desired by the community. The community is capable of educating itself.

SELF-REGULATING INFORMATION SYSTEMS

Education is information processing for the explicit purpose of reducing uncertainty. Social formations such as a government hierarchical society or a horizontally organized tribal community can be characterized as open, self-regulating systems which process information. Cybernetics, the science of such systems, reveals the great difference in the capacity of these two types of system to undertake the task.[45]

Vertical, hierarchical information systems maintain order by exercising authority. These systems are combinations of limitations which inhibit the flow of information through vested interests, with the ultimate result of producing limited decisions for action.

Horizontal, self-organizing information systems introduce order without authority and have an infinite capacity for new combinations, by communication through shared interests which motivate a high creative potential. Such systems are capable of coping with complex and unpredictable environments by producing optimal decisions for action.

It is of interest that the field of management was first motivated to promote research on the nature of communication systems. Vertical structures perpetuate social domination and dependence relationships. The concept of public participation is an invention of the oppressors, touted by governments and international development agencies. To *mobilize* public opinion and to *create* public awareness are expressions of ignorance in the field of human communication. What is public participation?

THE PICTURE AS AN IMITATIVE REPRODUCTION OF REALITY

Accepting the premise that only the community can educate itself, a number of interesting questions emerge. What would bring the community to desire social transformation? What kind of information would represent a reduction of uncertainty for the community? Bearing in mind that the transformation would initiate change from an oral to a written or from a predominantly imitative to a predominantly digital way of communication, what means of information processing would be appropriate and acceptable to the community?

Such swollen phrases as 'spiritual development' and 'conscientization of the individual' do not contribute to our understanding of the issue and are best avoided. The question can be rephrased, as: What medium may enable the community to evaluate its own reality in a way that will precipitate new judgements or formulations about it? What medium will trigger in the community a dialogue about its reality that will possibly lead to decisions and actions to alter that reality?

In my experience, the issue of literacy and social transformation must start with the picture—the imitative reproduction of reality. By picture, I mean the photograph or any picture having a photographic capacity in its reproduction of reality. Consideration of mystic, aesthetic or artistic viewpoints of what constitutes a picture of reality is unessential to this discussion. A sweating woman carrying a heavy water bucket on her head is precisely that in the picture and in reality. This information can be clearly communicated.

LINKING ORAL AND WRITTEN LIFESTYLES

With reference to our discussion in earlier chapters, the significance of the picture can be placed in perspective. It is the link between the oral and the written lifestyle and the first step on the way to the written abstraction. In other words, the picture is a bridge from a basically imitative to a digital mode of communication. Through structural likeness, the picture introduces the concept of regularity or repetitiveness in reality.

There is event A in reality and there is the picture of event A—which is like it. In a pedagogical sense, the picture starts with what is known in magic thinking, i.e. likeness. When you live *in* reality, sometimes you are not able to see it. The picture lifts the mind out of reality. Literally, you can hold reality and look at it from the outside. The picture makes an event into an object. In the world of magic there are no objects, because all objects are events.

Once the concept of the picture is established, once the mind is lifted out of reality, the next step is to link the first written concept, the word, to the picture. The picture is the visual environment of the word. The next step is the use of the word in its language environment, the sentence.

SEEING THE SAME THING

The picture helps to focus the attention of every person in the community.

It makes people 'see the same thing'. Because the picture is an object, people can more easily interact with it. The picture is closer to village people's imitative memory than the written word. The picture objectifies the inner 'seeing of the spirit'. The problem of transforming oral to written concept formation is that, in oral societies, people are more accustomed to verbalizing what they do than what they see.

THE COMMUNITY CONCEPT

What kind of a picture? Which pictorial concept will engender a process whereby people take a new look at their own reality? The content of a pictorial concept should be taken from the daily activities of people in the community. This is the basis of the community concept. The pictorial concept of water is not the picture of a lake or a bucket of water. It is the picture of a sweating woman carrying a water jar on her head. The pictorial concept of work is not so much the picture of a man chopping wood with an axe as it is the picture of a woman pounding maize or weeding the maizefield. Conceptual and social transformation are the same. Both can come about only through knowledge of social domination.

Who should produce the picture? The community should—not in the sense of actually drawing or reproducing it—there are photographic and reproduction methods available today which are inexpensive and efficient—but in the sense of deciding the picture's motif or theme.

'Mama Enifa and Mama Mande, show me how a woman cooks *nzima*.' The role of the photographer is to be the instrument which records and objectifies the visual reality, the visual image of the event of cooking *nzima*. The community provides the motif.

No one should decide in advance what the village community needs to know. Ask people, very often they know what they need to know.

ACTION WITH A PICTURE

The following account reveals how a group of women in Northern Province, Zambia, acted with a picture and started to look at their own reality.

Field worker: What is this?
Group: No answer.
Field worker: What do you see here on the wall? (pointing) Look!
Group: No answer.
Field worker: It is very dark here. Mama Mulenga, come close to the wall and tell the others what you see.
Mama Mulenga: . . . I see a picture.
Field worker: That's right, what do you see in the picture?
Mama Mulenga: . . . I see a woman.
Field worker: That's right, and what is the woman doing?
Mama Mulenga: . . . The woman is walking.

Field worker: That's right, the woman is walking. (to the others) What else is the woman doing?

Nakulu Mande: . . . The woman is carrying water.

Mama Mulenga (joining in): . . . The water jar is heavy . . .

Field worker: That's right, can you see which village the woman is from, which tribe does she belong to?

Mama Mulenga: The woman is like Bemba woman with *chitenga* . . .

Others (joining in): The woman has walked long way . . . The woman is tired . . . She has walked the hill from the river . . .

Field worker: That's right, the water jar is heavy to carry. Do you think she could get help to carry it? What can we do about that?

The way from oral expression to the verbalizing of visual representation may be slow and cumbersome, particularly in village communities without much exposure to pictorial stimulation.

In the following chapter, we will endeavour to clarify the nature and relationship of pictorial representation and pictorial perception. Through this description, ways to facilitate the pace of transformation may be identified.

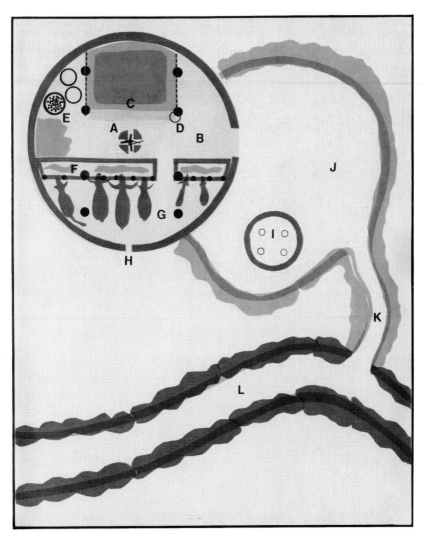

Village houses are neither untidy nor impractical. Like most huts in Africa, nothing is incidental in the Chaga hut on Mount Kilimanjaro. Each part has a spiritual and a practical function. A. Hearth. Of the two upper stones, one is called the husband's and the other the wife's. Each of the two corresponding posts are also named after them. B. The place for receiving visitors. C. Elevated section for the sleeping mats where no stranger is allowed. D. The post for sacrifice. E. Food and fodder store. F. Trough with railing. G. Cattle and goats. H. Drain. I. Staple storehouse. J. Yard with hedges. K. Winding passage for privacy. L. Public path.

A group of Maasai *morans*, young warriors, dancing their characteristic dance. The Maasai have a system of age groups; but there is no other social stratification and no central or hierarchical leadership. The priest, Oloiboni, must be consulted before all major decisions are taken. His authority, however, is based on the quality of his performance as an adviser. Western societies have much to learn from the social organization of the Maasai.

· One dwelling in the *manyatta*, where the young warriors remain for many years before they are considered ready for initiation and marriage. The counsellors of the group are selected at the beginning of their stay in the *manyatta*, later becoming the elders of the tribe. The community is profoundly egalitarian. Although women have access to the camp, they are not allowed to stay. Nowadays, they devote much of their time to producing jewellery for the tourists.

What do you see in the picture? . . . A woman cooking food. What kind of food is
the woman cooking? . . . The woman is cooking *nzima* (maize porridge). Why do
you think she is cooking *nzima*? . . . She is using a small pot. Are you sure she is
not cooking a relish? . . . The woman is cooking *nzima* . . . She is strewing mealie-
meal in the pot to make the *nzima* thicker!

Housewives cannot be fooled. They are quick to identify 'correct' domestic procedures. Visual aids should be based on their knowledge.

11
we see with our experience

'I shall call this figure the duck-rabbit. It can be seen as a rabbit's head or as a duck's. And I must distinguish between the "continuous seeing" of an aspect and the "dawning" of an aspect. The picture might have been shown me, and I have never seen anything but a rabbit in it.'
Ludwig Wittgenstein

THE FIGURE/BACKGROUND PHENOMENON

The digital structure of human language expressed in such phenomena as the negation and the dichotomy seems to be conditioned by the structure of our brain. Similarly, there are phenomena in our visual or pictorial perception which are structurally conditioned and therefore common to all people. Earlier, we discussed the principle of proximity and the gestalt idea of the good configuration. These phenomena are evidently at work in structuring our pictorial perception. Elements are perceived not in a disparate fashion but structured in wholes, based on circumstances such as proximity, likeness, configuration and regularity.

The figure/background phenomenon, however, appears to be congenitally determined. It is prominent in visual perception, but not limited to it. Sensory stimulation is perceived selectively in a preorganized pattern. Some stimulation comes to us in relief from a background of other stimulation. At this moment, my transistor radio is playing a popular melody. I perceive the saxophone clearly as something acoustically prominent in relation to the other instruments in the orchestra which provide a diffuse background. The figure/background phenomenon is related to the concepts of selective attention, focus and constancy. It is also affected by relative size and contrast, as we can see in the illustrations below.

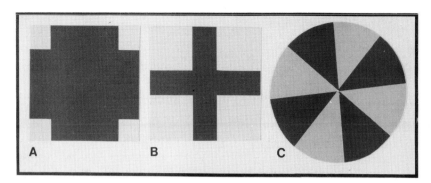

In A, there is a tendency to see light grey squares on a dark background. In B, there is a tendency to see a dark cross on a light background. In C, where the sizes are almost equivalent, the figure and background tend to alternate; we vacillate or flicker between seeing a dark fan on a light background or a light fan on a dark background. The important thing is that we always perceive one or the other. The figure part of the picture is something standing in relief against the background, something which gives the impression of more substance—although the picture is entirely flat print.

A similar perceptual phenomenon occurs in other shapes too.

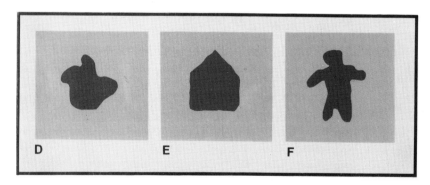

The spot in D stands out clearly as a dark grey configuration on a grey background. Even clearer is the phenomenon in E and F where the spots have a shape that indicates a meaning to the viewer, i.e. a house or a man.

Although it has important implications in the field of communications generally and in the field of cross-cultural communications in particular, little attention has been paid to the figure/background phenomenon. Later, we will assess its value in terms of layout and the design of pictorial material for communities with little or no exposure to pictorial stimulation.

First, however, the figure/background phenomenon should be linked to other phenomena in pictorial perception.

LEARNING TO READ PICTURES

There is a prevailing assumption that pictures as a mode of expression are universally understood. Many observations from the field confirm that this is not so. People learn to read pictures just as they learn to read the pages in a book. This is not recognized because education in reading pictures is an informal process. It goes on automatically in societies where a variety of pictures are presented daily through a variety of media. The television screen and the cinema, books, newspapers, magazines, photographs and paintings are part of people's visual environment from birth to death. In social environments with no pictorial tradition or very few pictorial representations—the situation in remote African villages—the informal process of learning to read pictures simply does not occur.

Teaching aids with pictures have been used extensively in health and nutrition education. The effect, however, is unclear.

To an old woman in Luapula, Zambia, I gave a picture handout of a woman breastfeeding her baby. The handout was A4 in size and printed on glossy art paper. We asked the old woman what she saw on the paper. She seemed not to understand the question. Instead, she lifted the picture to her nose, smelling it and feeling its smooth surface with her fingers. It was the intense whiteness of the paper, its straight edges and sharp corners which attracted her. Obviously, for the moment, she simply did not see the picture because she was focusing completely on the paper itself, on this strange material rarely seen in her remote village.

We are inclined to interpret this situation as if the old woman were incapable of seeing the picture. Rather, we should recognize that people's ability to read pictures is correlated to the amount of pictorial stimulation to which they have been exposed in their social environment. The ability to interpret pictures is largely a consequence of urbanization and the subsequent introduction of media providing pictorial representations to traditional societies. Exceptions are found in cultures with a pictorial tradition.

PERCEPTION—A SELECTIVE FUNCTION

How does our pictorial perception work? How do we process sensory information? Like the computer, our brain and sensory system react to *difference*. Again, it is based on the very simple digital principle: information/no information, i.e. our senses transmit information about *change* in our environment. Attention to change is decisive for survival. Since the capacity of our brain is limited and cannot cope with all the available information in a given situation, it selects certain parts which are considered important. In other words, our perception is not a passive receiving of information, but an active and *selective* function. The previous discussion of concept formation showed that we are actively structuring our reality. Consequently, our attention ability is restricted. Every distinct and fo-

145

cused perception of a stimulus happens at the expense of other stimuli. What we perceive attentively impinges on our consciousness in an isolated way.

This does not mean that all other sensory impressions are lost. They form a vague background with more or less distinctive details. This provides us with a deeper understanding of the figure/background phenomenon in visual perception. The principle of sensory selectivity explains why the old woman found the paper more interesting than the picture on it. To her, it was the material that represented a difference in sensory stimulation, not variations in the picture itself.

When our selective perception moves from the subconscious to the conscious, it is called purposeful observation or concentration. Attention is our perceptual focusing on selective stimuli as a conscious action while background stimuli are being monitored continuously by our subconsciousness in a state of preparedness for sudden change or significant new information. In the forest, we would hear immediately the calling of our name or the sound of footsteps, however focused our attention is on the rattling of a snake. Our higher mental processes tell us what is relevant for selection. With reference to the importance of difference and change to our organism, some physical properties of the stimuli possess greater importance than others.

Intensity, size, contrast and movement are the attention-getters. This is particularly evident in visual perception. Internal factors such as motivations, expectations, habits and attitudes also determine which stimulus is selected for attention. There is truth in the saying: You see what you are looking for. Perception is an active search for the interpretation of sensory information most meaningful to our organism. This interpretation includes an active application of our knowledge of the objects. With regard to our visual sense, it is relevant to say that we see with our experience.

CONSTANCY IN PERCEPTION

That experience and memory are greatly involved in our visual perception is indicated by various constancy phenomena. We display a tendency to see objects at a constant colour intensity despite variations due to different light and shade conditions.

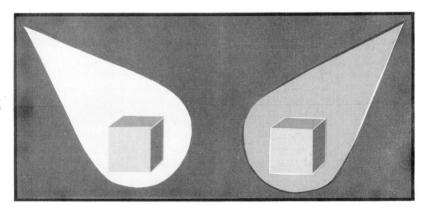

Colour constancy is dependent, among other things, on memory-colour.

Shape constancy refers to the tendency of an object to retain its shape in our perception even if the object is transformed in front of our eyes, for example a window which is swinging open.

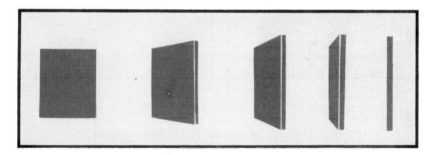

When we approach the window, it is rectangular; as we open it, it progresses through a number of trapezoid shapes until we see only the side of the frame with the hinges. Throughout these changes, we perceive the window as rectangular, because we see it with our memory.

Size constancy refers to the size of an object remaining the same in our perception whether the object is near or far. It is as if we have a mechanism in the brain which corrects for distance.

Location constancy is our perception of the things around us as enduring. We 'know' the things are there whether we observe them or not. All these constancy phenomena appear related to the process of objectification in concept formation. We actively structure our reality by making objects manageable which are really in various stages of flux. The concepts of constancy, certainty and information are closely related.

Constancy phenomena are of obvious importance to an ability to orient ourselves in reality and to an ability to recognize reality in pictures. Since experience plays such a prominent role in people's perceptions, it must be considered in depth in our elucidation of cross-cultural communication. People will display differing perceptions of reality and differing abilities in the recognition of reality in pictures according to the physical and social nature of their particular environment.

C.M. Turnbull, an anthropologist who lived for a period of time with the BaMbuti in the Congo, recounts a story which dramatically illustrates this point.[46] He brought a tribesman for the first time from his village deep in the forest into open savannah. When the Mbuti tribesman saw a herd of buffalo grazing some miles away, he asked what kind of insects they were. When he was told they were buffaloes, he reacted with alarm and refused to believe it. As the Land Rover approached the herd, he observed the insects were growing steadily in size and thought that he was under a magic spell. The spell was, of course, his complete lack of perceptual experience with horizontal distance. His visual environment was the rain forest where giant trees are positioned closely and randomly.

STRUCTURING OF VISUAL PERCEPTION

Let us examine in more detail the proximity factor, the tendency to perceive objects or configurations as 'belonging to each other' if they are close in space. In pictorial perception, the proximity factor becomes a more complex phenomenon, as the following example illustrates.

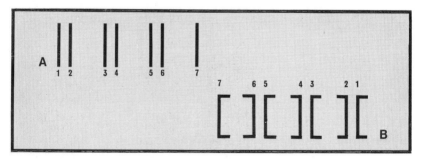

In row A, we automatically perceive the pattern as being 1—2, 3—4, 5—6, with 7 as an appendix. It is quite conceivable to structure row A in pairs 6—7, 4—5, 2—3, with 1 as an extra, but it simply does not come naturally to us.

In row B, the vertical lines are positioned at exactly the same distance from each other as in A, but a direction factor is introduced which completely alters our perception. We perceive the row as consisting of the pairs 7—6, 5—4, 3—2, with 1 as extra. In row B, the direction factor overrides the proximity factor as a dominant feature in our perception and literally creates 'a new picture'. This example demonstrates an important principle in pictorial perception, namely that detail determines our perception of the whole. Conversely, the properties of the whole also affect the ways in which details are perceived.

The structuring phenomenon in visual perception is, to some extent, observable in people. Following the eyes of a person who is looking at a picture, one observes how he scans the surface from detail to detail until the information is processed and an interpretation of the whole is integrated. People who have not learned to read and interpret details 'correctly' may mis-perceive and mis-interpret the entire picture.

A PICTURE IS NOT SQUARE

To understand better the use of visual aids, we should examine another aspect of visual perception. Contrary to our belief, the picture is not square. When the eye is fixed on a certain point in a picture and the picture is held at a certain distance from the eye, the picture for a split second actually appears as an oval. This can be illustrated by a very simple device as in Picture A below. The test person closes one eye and fixes the other on the cross-point. In all four directions from this point, a series of arbitrarily selected numbers are hidden under mobile strips of cardboard. The strips are moved slowly outwards, one by one. The test person is asked to identify the numbers which appear. After a while, the numbers disappear

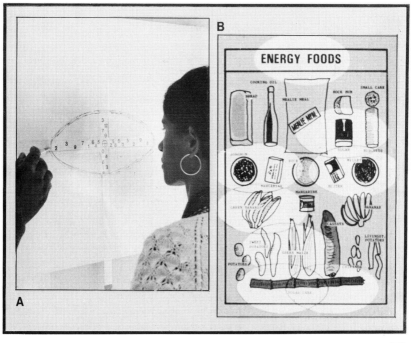

in the peripheral parts of the test person's vision and become unintelligible contrasts which finally disappear.

On the basis of this experiment, a rough oval can be drawn which indicates the field of vision at a given distance. The oval corresponds to the shape of the eyeball. In Picture B, we illustrate what is happening as the eye scans a picture. We can imagine how the eye moves over the chart in a series of split second oval fixations. This movement is determined by a series of factors such as intensity, contrast and shape. We can safely assume that these qualities registered by the periphery of the eye's retina are decisive in determining the direction the eye will take as it scans a picture. At a certain distance, if we perceive the teaching chart in B as rectangular, it is because we see with our experience. Our oval field of vision consists of zones.

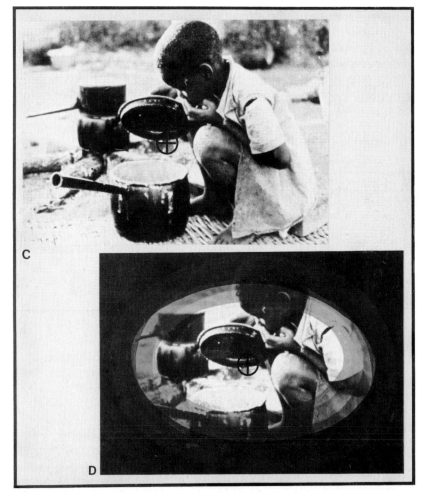

C

D

If we imagine Picture C to be considerably larger than the size of this page and we close one eye and focus the other on the cross-point, our field of vision appears as in D. The fixed cross-point is centred in the *fovea centralis* of the retina, the area of the eye having the clearest vision. From the *fovea centralis* the clarity of vision gradually diminishes towards the extremity of the retina, where only vague contrasts can be perceived. These peripheral contrasts and shapes are decisive for the eye's movements.

LAYOUT—HELPING TO SEE

From the point of view of developing communication aids, it is evident that the composition or layout is critical to a viewer's perception and comprehension of pictures, teaching aids, printed information material and films. Layout is a functional tool which should make the reader or viewer see what is intended to be seen in the picture. It is not an artistic or photographic gimmick.

GESTALT AND VALENCE

Although the movements of the eye are determined by physical details in the field of vision, other factors play a significant role. In studying the relationship between the details and the whole of a picture, the Gestalt psychologists observed that some details assume greater importance in our

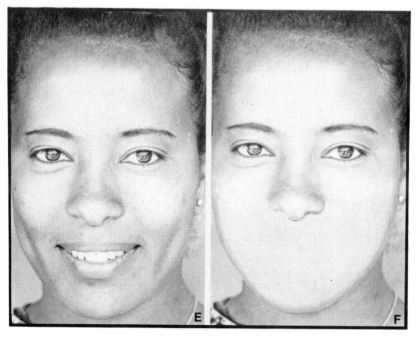

perception of the whole than others.[47] The quality of importance of the detail they called *valence*. In our perception of a face, as in photographs E/F, the smiling mouth has an extremely high valence — much higher than the chin or even the nose.

If either of these were missing, but the mouth remained, we would still perceive the essential expression of the entire face. This is not so when the mouth is the missing detail.

Modern electronics make it possible to demonstrate this in another way. A light-spot is projected on the eye while it is looking at a picture. The light-spot is recorded by a TV camera and will move over the picture as the eye moves, registering the continuous eye movements. This can be super-

G

imposed on a TV screen and followed live. It can also be exposed on a photographic film. This happening will then appear as indicated in illustrations G/H.

The spot has moved on and off the eyes and the mouth; both are details possessing high valence in the perception of the personality of the picture. This is illustrative of the real life situation. Good person-to-person communication is dependent on eye contact and eye/mouth contact, although this is not necessarily true in all cultures. We process information about another person largely by scanning his or her eyes and facial expressions. In the picture, the focus also wanders to other areas—and a beauty spot is certainly a detail which has a good reason for its reputation!

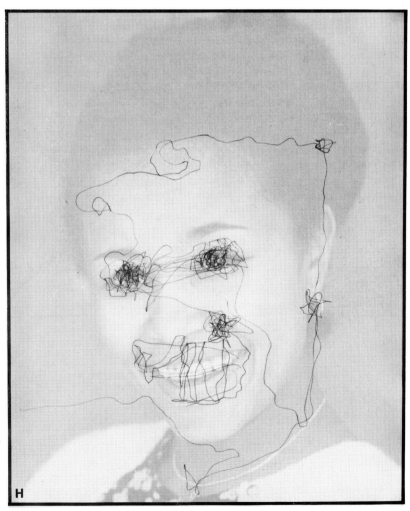

H

A PICTORIAL LANGUAGE

The details of a picture form a kind of pictorial language. Certain details play the part of nominals or nouns (objects) while other details represent the predication or the verb (the action). The relationship between the details is the syntax (the whole). We can say this language consists of a series of cues which people must know in order to be able to perceive and interpret correctly the content or message of a picture. Therefore, people must acquire a technique to be able to process information from pictures as it is intended. As a corollary, pictures cannot be used as efficient means of communication unless the producer of the picture knows and can apply the pictorial language and, above all, has an assessment of the language knowledge of his audience.

PICTURE READING—INFORMAL EDUCATION

As mentioned initially in this chapter, it is important to realize that pictorial literacy—the ability to read pictures, i.e. to process information from a pictorial representation—is the result of an informal educational process. This skill probably develops in proportion to the amount of pictorial stimulation to which the individual is exposed in his environment. Some environments, such as the rural village in many parts of the world, are deficient in pictorial stimulation. As a consequence, good picture readers do not emerge in the rural village. In environments where stone is the only available building material, people develop better skills as stonemasons than as carpenters. And in societies inundated with various forms of pictorial stimulation, people acquire the ability to process the given information from pictures. Picture reading is a practical skill.

THREE DIMENSIONS EXPRESSED IN TWO DIMENSIONS

A basic problem in pictorial perception is that a three-dimensional reality

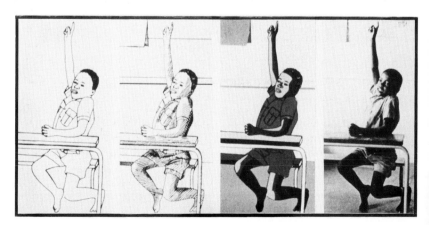

has to be expressed in two dimensions. The fourth dimension, the time factor, further complicates the matter, entering the picture when the expression of movement is depicted. Depth, the third dimension, is expressed by various cues. One is the shade-cue. Shade-cues can be reproduced in different ways, ranging from line-hatching to photographic tones. They provide the knowledgeable reader with the cue to depth in the picture.

The line drawing to the left has no such texture and therefore provides no depth cue.

In my experience, photographs convey information about reality more effectively than line drawings. This derives from the fact that the variations of density in texture in shaded areas are photochemically reproduced and therefore provide cues which are very close to the cues provided by the light conditions in a three-dimensional reality.

RELATIVE SIZE

Other depth cues in a picture are provided by *relative size* and relative height in the horizontal plane. These are illustrated in various versions of the pictures below. For those unfamiliar with this cue, it is perfectly logical to say that they see some people in the picture who are giants and some who are midgets. After a woman from Barotseland in Zambia had viewed similar pictures, she said, 'I see big people and very small people.' Beyond that she had no perception, or could or would not express a perception, of what was happening in the picture.

THE PERSPECTIVE CUE

It is important to understand that perspective is nothing more than a pictorial or artistic convention which appeared in European painting as late as the Renaissance. Before that time, paintings were flat, without cues for spatial relationships. Perspective is a visual illusion based on the linear geometrical notion that two parallels meet at the horizon. Perspective is one of the most important cues to perception of depth and distance and thereby to the sizes of objects in pictures.

In the lake-side picture, perspective gives us the clue to the considerable length of the two logboats, however little we actually see of them. The lines of the road in the other picture provide a clue to the spatial area in which the women are moving. People from a western culture interpret perspective cues as a matter of course. They do not realize that the cues may be incomprehensible to people who have not learned to read them. Several teachers at technical colleges and vocational training centres have pointed out to me the problem this poses. Basically, it is the incongruity of using the inevitable blueprints or work drawings of modern technology as introductory learning material for students coming from social environments where pictorial stimulation is minimal.

SUPERIMPOSITION, ANOTHER CUE

Superimposition is a cue linked to perception of depth and distance. If one object or body covers another, or a number of others, the interpretation is that the first is nearer in the pictorial space. To some degree this assump-

tion is self-evident. Despite its simplicity, the superimposition cue is significant in understanding pictures.

All the cues described are concerned with the problem of perceiving three-dimensional objects and depths of space on a two-dimensional surface. That this occurred must be lauded as one of the major innovations in the technology of pictorial representation. The pictorial cues illustrate my contention that they constitute a pictorial language, a method for the processing of pictorial information which must be acquired before pictorial messages can be understood.

CONTRADICTORY INFORMATION

Like other languages, this language is not meaningful if it communicates contradictory information. This illustration

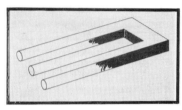

serves to prove that point. It sends incompatible spatial information to the retina, an extremely frustrating experience because the brain cannot finally decide on an interpretation. Pictorial cues are simply social conventions. From this point of view, it is clear we see as much with our experience as we see with our eyes. In the above illustration, there is a conflict between what we see with our eyes and what we see with our experience.

OTHER CUES

The *movement cue* deserves mention. In general, when we perceive movement, we perceive it as action in space taking place over time. When this is transferred to a two-dimensional still picture, it is evidently not possible to preserve much of the event. The movement cue, therefore, is mainly based on the fact that we see with our experience. We know from experience that bodies or objects in movement take certain relative positions. The man chopping down a tree provides us with a cue by the position in which he holds the axe. The track runner provides us with a movement cue in the position of his legs.

A person who has not learned to read the cues of frozen movement would say that the figure in the picture has lost one of his legs. This is a perfectly logical interpretation and was repeatedly expressed when this picture was shown in rural areas.

Finally, we have what could be termed *identification cues.* These are an infinite number of cues which make it possible for us to recognize objects and physical events in pictures. These cues are based on the likeness between the picture and the person or object portrayed or photographed.

The track runner is a suitable example. The human body has several identification cues—two arms, two legs, a head, etc. There is a limit to the number of cues that can be absent before it becomes impossible to identify the object as a running man.

It is reasonable to assume that if all these cues are present and clearly exposed in the picture, it is easier to recognize the object than if only a few are present.

IMAGE AND VISUAL IDENTITY

The concept 'seeing with our experience' relates more specifically to perceptual phenomena such as the constancy phenomena, i.e. that objects retain their size or shape in our perception even if their position changes in relation to us. The reader will appreciate that these phenomena are closely connected with what is called the image, i.e. the visual identity of objects. This concept is synonymous with the concept of the Gestalt. In addition to the idea that a number of identification cues characterize an object, we must recognize that through our experience of an object, cues acquire a qualitative aspect. This is why some cues are more important than others or have a higher valence in the perception of identifying the object as a whole.

Even an experienced reader of pictures has to look twice before he recognizes the objects in the biggest picture. So many of the identity cues are omitted and the remainder are projected so unclearly that a deliberate and concentrated study is required before the content can be assessed. The man with his back to the viewer, playing the Zambian chess game *nsolo* on the ground, is another example. In the picture of the small girl taken from below, some of the identification cues are so distorted that

they require considerable effort to decipher. The picture of the two hands
with a cooking pot and a wooden spoon is an example of the confusion
that can be created when the relationship between identification cues—
the details and their context—is incomplete. Often we see what we are
looking for. The sophisticated picture reader may find that elimination or
distortion of identification cues increases the artistic expression of a picture. From a communication point of view, distortion is an obstacle to perception. These pictures all present various types of obstacles to the perception of their message. For a person with little experience of pictures, it is
puzzling to see a solitary pair of hands floating in space, holding a cooking
pot and a wooden spoon. During one village test, women had difficulty
perceiving the content of this close cut. When the picture of the entire woman holding the pot was shown, perception was made easier. People who
are accustomed to western picture-editing of film and television, where
close cuts are a prevalent feature, are not disposed to consider alternative
editing techniques.

RELEVANT VISUAL EXPERIENCE

The fact that experience plays such a dominant role in our perception implies that people cannot be expected to identify objects they have never
experienced. This simple fact has obvious implications for the use of pictures in a cross-cultural context. The frequent practice of teaching nutri-

tion in Africa with foreign pictures of steaks or canned fruits is an exercise in irrelevance.

What is a house? As the reader can see from these pictures, that depends entirely on the cultural context of the viewer.

We must assume that the more relevant the pictured objects are to the experiences of a person's daily life, the easier it is for the reader to identify them. The picture of the nun walking into the Roman arch has only a few identification cues, but the visual image, the gestalt, will be perceived very strongly by those who have had that relevant visual experience.

PERCEPTION—STRUCTURING OF A WHOLE

What happens in the perceptual process? This question is central to the composing of a picture. Remembering that perception is a process in which we actively structure reality, we can delineate the split-second process in the following way: First perceived are the identification of rough contrasts and basic shapes (1). Then attention is suddenly focused on a few details with high valence (2), such as facial features and hands in action. Following the perception of these details, the picture is structured further (3). New cues are read which add to the interpretation of the whole and, finally, the picture appears as a structured and meaningful whole (4). The achievement of the last stage depends on the degree of pictorial reading experience of the perceiving person. As stipulated, this will vary with the amount of pictorial stimulation to which a person has been exposed.

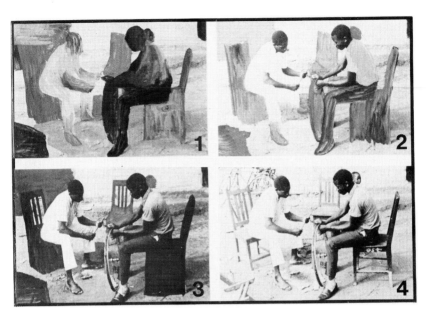

DIFFERENT SKILLS IN VISUAL PERCEPTION

Envisage a continuum of experience in reading pictures, from a person with no skills in pictorial perception as a result of no stimulation to a person highly skilled as a result of continuous exposure to various types of pictorial stimulation. The following visual fabrication illustrates the situation.

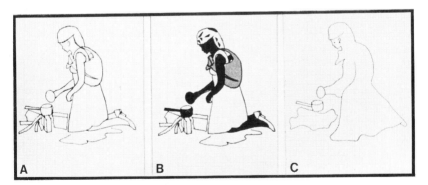

The line drawing in A is a good starting point because line drawings are poor reproductions of reality, requiring considerable pictorial experience to be perceived and interpreted correctly. When an experienced person perceives A, he automatically and subconsciously reads more into the drawing than is actually there. He sees it, literally, with his experience: the fireplace and the bundle on the back provide cues that make him interpret the picture as one of an African woman. Hence, he infers that she has a dark complexion. The bundle on her back is usually a different colour from her dress, the headwear has a rich design, and the cooking pot is black. In other words, he reads substance in between the lines of the drawing. He gives flesh to it. Subconsciously he adds to it and his final perception of A is more like B.

Conversely, the person having little experience with pictures and, therefore, limited picture reading skills will misperceive or perceive less information than is actually provided. Since he would have difficulty identifying picture details in general and probably line drawings in particular, he is likely to see the picture as presented in C. Identified are a few details with high valence, such as the facial features or the familiar shape of the cooking pot, but the whole remains perceptually an unstructured heap of lines.

THE STUDY OF PERCEPTION IN LINE DRAWINGS

A study of perception in line drawings has been carried out among village people in some rural areas of Kenya.[48] Line drawings have been extensively used in visual aids for the purpose of health and nutrition education. This study confirms the above assumptions in applying this pictorial style and demonstrates how the pictorial inexperience of the rural villager may lead him to incomplete perception or misperception of a picture. Village people scan a picture perceiving its details one by one. This allows a gradual process of structuring the information until an interpretation is achieved. The process is indirectly demonstrated in the results of the study. In the following selection of animal pictures, most people were able to identify accurately the cow, the chicken, the bird, the dog and the cat.

On average, 70—80 per cent of the village people managed to give the correct name. Some 'incorrect' answers for the cat were the interpretations leopard, lion and hyena. The drawing of the cat creates ambiguity through its inaccurate rendition of detail and anatomical proportion, making these alternative interpretations viable. In this case, the results simply indicate that the people were brighter than the artist. Twenty-seven per cent of the respondents did not identify the fish, whereas the snake was identified by almost 100 per cent. The first is not common in daily life, while the latter exists in the environment and carries strong emotional connotations.

Horses are not indigenous to Africa, surviving only in certain areas. About 60 per cent could not identify the horse. However, this lack of recognition seems also related to a significant detail—the lowered position of the horse's head in the drawing. It is much easier to identify a horse with a raised neck. Apparently, that posture is more representative of the image of a horse in most people's experience.

The goat and the tortoise posed a very special problem. Approximately 50 per cent of the people could identify the goat. According to the report, it became obvious to the interviewers that the subjects were scanning the details of the drawing and recognizing them one by one. The drawing as a complete object was not looked at initially. The tail was the detail which confused so many of the villagers, making them call the goat a cow. Obviously the drawing was wrong in its depiction of this detail. Goats have tails that turn upwards! Although the tortoise was identified by more people, approximately 30 per cent answered incorrectly. The answers emphasize the importance of the careful attention to clues which is necessary for the process of correct interpretation of the whole. Those for whom the head determined the interpretation of the picture identified the tortoise as a snake. Others concentrated on the legs and called it an elephant. The pattern of the carapace gave some the idea that it was a crocodile. Considering the circumstances, these interpretations are all equally sensible and valid.

Interpretations of another set of drawings of common objects used in the same study adds confirmation to the importance of detail in the perception of an entire picture.

Recognizing that people without picture reading skills would not be able to interpret the perspective cues, it is not surprising that 30-40 per cent of them failed to identify the table and the chair. For some respondents, the drawings were probably just a heap of lines. They were not able to build substance into the lines of the drawing. Another factor may be the rare occurrence in daily life of the object itself. The cupboard yielded a more interesting result. Among rural villagers, the recognition was as low as 8 per cent! Again, with lack of knowledge of perspective cues and relative size cues, it is understandable that the drawing was often interpreted as a church or a school. The panels in the doors are a striking detail which, disregarding their position, resemble the rows of wooden

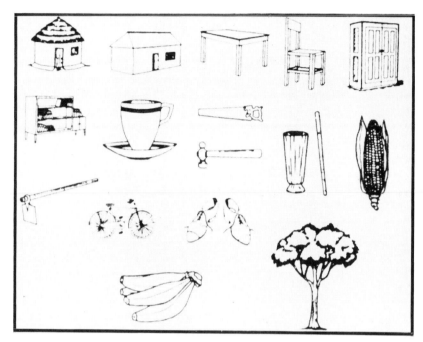

benches found in churches and schools in rural areas. Consequently, this detail determined the perception of the whole picture. Admittedly, it is not a very naturalistic drawing of a cupboard.

The drawing of the mortar and the pestle produced some remarkable reactions. Although the mortar and pestle are among the most common objects found in rural areas, only about 20 per cent of the villagers could identify them. The details literally spoil the perception of the picture. The pestle is completely out of proportion to the mortar and, in real life, would never stand on its own as it does in the drawing. If the pestle had been standing in the mortar or had been lying on the ground beside it, correct identification would have been facilitated.

Interpretation of the hoe produced fresh astonishment. Almost 50 per cent failed to identify it, possibly because the hoe depicted does not resemble those commonly used in the areas where the test was conducted and because hoes are seldom seen at this angle to the horizontal. Some villagers identified the drawing of the hoe as a man walking along a road. For an attentive observer, this detail exists. The blade has a little head, with a V-shaped neck in the shirt, and the lines of the handle create the visual illusion of a road. This is, detail by detail, a sensible interpretation. Readers are missing the point by thinking these interpretations are strange or funny.

IMPORTANCE OF DETAILS

The Kenyan study also investigated line drawings in a more comparative way. The results add further confirmation to the importance of the detail for the correct interpretation of the whole.

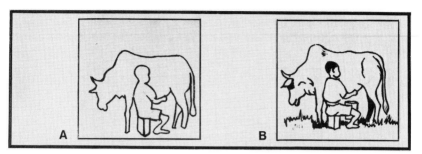

In the above illustrations, picture A is schematic and contains a minimum of detail. It was correctly recognized by 71 per cent. The incorrect answers were a donkey and milking a rhino. The latter answer is a viable alternative as the profile of the cow's head really seems to include the horn of a rhinoceros. In picture B, where more realistic descriptive detail was included, the correct answers increased to 88 per cent (man milking or milking a cow).

Low figures for correct recognition may indicate that some drawings simply were not well conceived as pictures of objects in reality. Low figures also raise the question of the suitability of line drawings as a graphic style for cross-cultural visual aids. Line drawings are abstract in their way of describing objects. They provide the viewer with the outline of an object but not the substance, a tangible, visible quality found in a photograph or a naturalistic painting.

READING THE PERSPECTIVE CUE

The results of other studies of the perspective cue confirm that people inexperienced in pictorial interpretation do not pay attention to this cue. This does not necessarily mean that such a cue is not *seen*. Rather, it implies that the perspective cue is not interpreted.

In drawing C, the perspective cue is given by the converging lines of the road. The test was performed among migrant South African mine workers who could not read or write. The correct answer to the question 'What is the man in the picture doing?' was 'Man spearing buck, impala, antelope.' Incorrect answers were 'Man spearing elephant, pig.' More than 91 per cent of the workers misinterpreted the cue, as they did also in picture D where the perspective is indicated by superimposition of objects and size cues. However significant the results seem, one may ask if they are not as indicative of the unsuitability of line drawings in pictorial communication as of the skills of the respondents.

PHOTOGRAPH OF A 'HEALTHY' BOY

To show the ramifications of using photographs as visual aids in cross-cultural communication, some observations I made in Zambia about reactions to a photograph of the face of a young, healthy boy are useful. The intention was to use the photo of a smiling, healthy and contented boy for nutrition education. The approach was very similar to the westernized toothpaste advertising style—a strong face, fresh from a rain shower. The picture was tested on approximately 50 pedestrians in Lusaka who, presumably, had been exposed to some pictorial stimulation by their presence in the city. About 70 per cent clearly identified the object. Given the purpose of the picture, the more subtle interpretations were finally considered more important. Some said: 'He has a skin disease.' The rain drops were perceived as blisters. 'He has the beginning of leprosy.' The highlights on the nose and both cheeks were seen as palish skin changes or peelings. 'He is blind' or 'He has eye disease.' The white highlight spots in the eyes were seen as trachoma or a similar distortion of the eye. 'He has a strange front tooth.' The shadow between the front teeth was lacking. These interpretations confirm that the detail is decisive to the interpretation of the whole.

PRACTICAL SKILLS IN READING PICTURES

Caution should be exercised in the interpretation of these studies—which are attempting an assessment not of people's intelligence but of their practical skill in reading pictures. If a person does not reply that the picture of a tortoise is 'a tortoise', it cannot be inferred that the person is incapable of seeing the tortoise. More probably, the person has not yet developed the skill, i.e. acquired the perceptual habit, of integrating the details provided in a whole which, by social convention, is considered correct. Pictures are conventions conditioned by the cultures from which they emerge. They are not a cross-cultural universal language independent of people's experience. If pictures are to play a role in cross-cultural communication, it is necessary to develop a pictorial language functionally adjusted to people's experience.

THE FIGURE/BACKGROUND STUDY

The above conclusion led me, in 1969, to undertake a small pilot study on

picture styles in Zambia.[49] The study was addressed to the utilization of the figure/background phenomenon with various reproduction styles, such as line drawing, silhouette and photograph. Assuming that the relevance of objects and pictures to people's daily life and environment is decisive for their proper recognition, the following motifs were photographed at random: a walking lion; a woman sitting cooking *nzima*; a woman walking with a bucket on her head; a cooking pot on a charcoal burner; a man drinking beer; a kettle on a fireplace; a house with a woman sitting outside. All these motifs are very familiar to most Zambians in any part of the country. The photographs were enlarged to 10 x 16 inches and copies were produced in the following picture styles: (1) a simple line drawing; (2) a silhouette; (3) a block-out of the subject, i.e. with the background eliminated from the photograph; and (4) a photograph. Some of the series of pictures in these different styles are presented below.

The study was conducted among women and men who had been exposed to little pictorial stimulation and who could not read or write. Most of the people were from rural areas. In total, 63 people were interviewed according to the following procedure. The pictures were presented to one person at a time, in a series of four held in a half circle so that the distance to the eyes should be equal. Great care was taken that the order of the pictures from left to right was altered in a random manner for each series of four. As in the illustration, a table was usually found to support the photographs. After seeing the series, each subject was asked the following question in his or her language: 'These four pictures show you the same thing, tell you the same story: can you tell us what you see?' When the respondent's verbal identification of the content was correct or satisfactory, we asked: 'Will you point out in which picture you saw this first?' During the interview, the eye and head movements of the respondent were observed carefully. With few exceptions, the eye movements indicated the same picture as the one finally pointed out by the respondent. The results of the study are presented in the following table.

Number of identifications in different picture styles

Picture Series	Line drawing	Silhouette	Block-out	Photo-graph
Walking lion	1	3	37	15
Woman sitting cooking	4	3	35	19
Woman with bucket on head	3	0	36	22
Cooking pot on charcoal burner	2	5	39	15
Man drinking beer	0	7	30	20
Kettle on fireplace	2	6	23	16
House with woman	3	6	30	21
Total	15	30	230	128

For practical reasons, not all the respondents were given all the tests. Only two out of a total of 63 subjects failed to identify as well as to point to any picture at all. One person interpreted the house as an elephant. No significant difference resulted from the variation in the motifs selected.

Line drawings elicited the lowest response and a very low point-out value. The simple form in which they were presented for the test did not seem to supply the observer with the amount of detail necessary for identification and interpretation of the whole. Also, line drawings did not attract attention by contrast.

Silhouettes produce a slightly stronger impact than line drawings. This higher response does not result from more detail being provided but is probably due to the stronger contrast in the silhouette style relative to the other visual presentations. There are constraints on the kind of content which can be expressed graphically in the silhouette manner.

Block-outs produced the overwhelming majority of point-outs. Through their figure/background composition, block-outs provide good contrast. At the same time, details and cues of the motifs are registered by the photographic lens in a manner which facilitates identification and understanding. Rendering of detail is further accentuated by the completely neutral background where all details interfering with the essential pictorial message are eliminated.

Photographs received a high level of response, but not as high as the block-outs. Photographic background providing details extraneous to the message only creates interference and subsequent confusion. Even though the background detail in the test photograph was minimal and neutral, it was obviously a detracting factor in communicating the intended message.

I concluded the report of this study with the following remarks:

Although there is ample reason for repeating this study under more systematic and better-controlled conditions, it can hardly be denied that it gives strong indications regarding the suitability of the picture styles which were comprised in it. Nor should the artistic and functional reasons from the layout viewpoint, which I have outlined earlier, be underestimated. The 'block-out' is preferred much more than the line drawing because it is a functionally much better solution.

ANOTHER STUDY IN NEPAL

In 1975, the study was repeated by a team from the National Development Service (NDS) and UNICEF in Nepal. About 400 villagers from various remote parts of the country were the respondents.[50] Regarding picture styles, the study extended the series from four to six by including a three-tone drawing similar in effect to a photograph and a highly stylized almost isometric drawing.

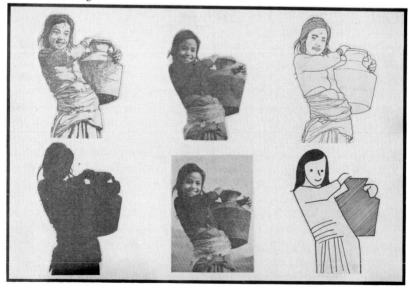

From the illustrations, it is evident that these six pictures of a girl with a water jar were artistically and technically excellent. The rate of response was as follows. The three-tone drawing was recognized by 72 per cent, the block-out photograph by 67 per cent, the line drawing by 62 per cent, the silhouette by 61 per cent, the photograph by 59 per cent and the stylized drawing by 49 per cent. The results indicate that the principle of the block-out can be applied in several pictorial styles. It can be used photographically or as a three- or four-tone line drawing in ink pen, or as a wash with an infinite number of tones by brush. If there are limitations to the printing facilities, the last two methods will give better reproduction than a photographic block-out. However, artists who can deliver the necessary technical quality are probably too expensive and produce too slowly when large numbers of drawings are required. It seems that the use of a competent photographer is, ultimately, the most inexpensive way of producing large quantities of pictures. Light-setting that creates good contrast in the photograph is the best way to solve printing problems.

PEOPLE ARE FAST LEARNERS

In conclusion, we should emphasize that problems of pictorial perception are sometimes exaggerated. Generally, people are very fast learners. There is no reason to relate these phenomena in pictorial perception specifically to people from the Third World who cannot read or write and who are unaccustomed to pictures. The figure/background phenomenon is a universal human perceptual feature. To utilize this principle functionally in a layout or a photograph is the object of any professionally alert and observant graphic artist. The message of the picture is rendered easier to perceive for any group of people, whether they are villagers or post-graduate students. Our concern with cross-cultural communication in traditional communities generally or in the field of health and nutrition particularly will be discussed in the context of functional visual aids after first attempting to understand with more empathy the traditional community itself.

12
community health

'How are you today, Kamanga?'
'I am a bit all right, sir.'
'I see . . . is anything wrong, then?'
*'I am sick, Bwana, my friend Staxon talks
much bad about me.'*

OPPRESSION BY PROFESSIONALISM

The western-educated medical doctor practising in the African village is, for all his good intentions and good results, an example of oppression by professionalism. That the oppression is often unwitting does not make it less suspect as a human relationship. It is the example of the professional so preoccupied with his knowledge that he can see only the ignorance of others. Platitudes expounded in the name of professionalism include: child malnutrition is a disease caused by the ignorance and poverty of the mother; the mother's lack of cleanliness causes diarrhoea. Ignorance and poverty remain undefined, but the diagnosis is considered precise and mothers are prescribed a shot of health education or a dose of nutrition lessons.

Primary health care and nutritional improvement are emerging as high priority issues in the process of social transformation in Third World countries. Those who work with people in rural villages or urban neighbourhoods recognize the potential of these issues for improving the quality of life. Health and nutritional status are seemingly measurable concepts, but they have social and cross-cultural implications which require elaboration.

HEALTH—WELL-BEING OF THE COMMUNITY

In affluent societies, clinical and preventive medicine is focused on the comfort and well-being of the individual. Health has become distorted to the practising of a concept in which people are consumers of medical treatments. Almost exclusively, health is measured by the physical state of the human body. By and large, health is produced for consumers by the definitions offered by the medical establishment and by the vested interests of the pharmaceutical industry.

In an African village, health is a more comprehensive concept. Certainly it concerns a person's body, but equally it concerns a person's relationship to other people. This relationship extends to the family and the wider circle of the clan and the tribe as well as ancestors and spirits. Health is not an individual matter. It is a matter of a person's well-being in the context of the community. This is why Kamanga genuinely feels sick when his friend thinks badly of him. Community health is a concept in medical terminology requiring reassessment.

PRODUCTION OF SOCIAL RELATIONS

Community health can be better understood by comparing the fundamental differences in the value systems and lifestyles of a western and an African community. In the modern urban community, people are oriented to individual performance and achievement. They produce material goods and services and the process is one of high productivity. The reward accompanying achievement is an improvement in material living standards.

In the rural setting, people have other values. They are certainly interested in good food and material comfort, but more as a communal concern. People's real desire is to produce good and lasting social relations. What seems to an observer to be endless time idled away around the *boma*, under the tree or in the bar is highly productive time from the viewpoint of this value system. The subsistence community is a social formation on the edge of fragility. People know it; they also know the weakness of human nature. Great effort is needed to keep the delicate balance between individual needs and community interests. Agreements must be made and alliances forged. Grudges must be aired and claims settled. One thing is certain, no one survives without the survival of the community.

THE SOCIAL ETIQUETTE

The fundamental difference in value systems—one emphasizing the material and the other emphasizing the social—is illustrated touchingly in a simple daily convention, the greeting. Whereas the atmosphere in the urban western community is abrupt and sometimes abrasive, the rural African community has retained elaborate social manners and a high degree of politeness. The African form of address is polite and considerate, especially between close relatives, and clearly deferential in relation to elders. Politeness is a social device which minimizes the chances of friction in face-to-face relationships. There is a universal social accord which stipulates that politeness as a code of behaviour should be met reciprocally. Detailed rules prescribe how husbands, wives, children, sons-in-law, daughters-in-law, grandparents, chiefs and friends of the house should behave in their respective social roles. Rules of permission and rules of avoidance are generally very elaborate. For example, a man (A) may behave freely with his brother's (B) wife. Should the brother (B) die, A will take B's wife as his own. In this way, the community provides social insurance. On the other hand, the degree of conversation a man is allowed with his mother-in-law is circumscribed for fear of her husband's wrath. These rules vary according to tribe. Unpleasant comments are made socially acceptable through circumlocutions. If you want to be impolite, you must accomplish it politely!

SHARING OF RESOURCES

Gift-giving is another important social convention in the traditional community. It carries the same expectation of mutuality and directly relates to a just distribution of resources within the community. Gift-giving is also governed by elaborate rules, particularly the sharing of food which reinforces respect and commitment to kinship bonds. Thus, politeness and gift-giving are social mechanisms which maintain community health and cohesion for the purpose of survival. These two major social conventions are found almost universally in subsistence societies.

In earlier chapters, these social phenomena have been discussed from other viewpoints. Now let us look at politeness and gift-giving as they relate to community health. For example, if a villager feels sick, he is almost certain to approach a healer with a chicken as a gift expressing deference to the healer's knowledge and status in society.

MODERN AND TRADITIONAL MEDICINE

Let us review some of the differences and similarities in the treatment of patients in modern and traditional medicine.

Only a small percentage of patients seeking treatment in western societies are actually suffering from a fatal or serious physical illness. Perhaps half of the patients have symptoms which can be attributed to a psychiatric origin. In addition, there are those patients with relatively minor ailments whose symptoms are disproportionately aggravated by the patient's anxieties. Lastly, there are patients suffering from small digestive disorders, minor infections and colds, which generally disappear without treatment. The proportion of seriously ill patients actually treated by the western practitioner is relatively small.

The pattern is very similar to the traditional herbalist or diviner in an African village. Here, however, an added dimension is that people suffer from a variety of diseases such as parasitic infections, fever and skin ailments which are generally more debilitating than immediately dangerous to people's lives.

In both situations, the illnesses and ailments of the majority of patients are such that they respond to a variety of treatments. We should be aware that in the field of both western and traditional medicine there are not enough conspicuous treatment failures to challenge the efficiency of or the belief in either system.[51] Modern medicine makes a decisive difference to a relatively small number of lives. Surgical and obstetric emergencies, acute infections and childhood diseases are the areas where modern medicine is infinitely superior. Traditional medicine seems incapable of dealing with the terrifying problem of infant mortality and epidemiological diseases.

THE 'HOW' AND THE 'WHY' OF DISEASE

Both the western and the traditional doctor examine, diagnose and treat their patients systematically. The success of western medicine is based on the detached scientific analysis of causal relationships. This analysis is made largely on the basis of statistical methods for the identification and description of the causes and symptoms of the average case of illness and its response to specific medications. This knowledge allows the modern clinician to diagnose and treat his patient as a 'case' with the focus on *how* the case occurred. By virtue of the methodology of the statistical average, the modern clinician is detached from his patient. The psychology of a sick person, however, disposes him or her to be peripherally interested in the 'how' of the disease. The overwhelming question for a sick person is: *Why* did I fall sick? Nor is the patient interested if his or her symptoms constitute a statistical average. On the contrary, for the patient, attention is focused on how his/her state of illness differs from that of others. Often, it is this state of mind that the traditional healer or diviner is more successful in exploring—and possibly in exploiting. Why did I fall sick? Have I offended one of my ancestors? Has an enemy cast a spell on me?

REDRESSING IMBALANCE IN THE SOCIAL ORDER

The interesting aspect of these questions is their consideration of illness as a condition related to the community as a whole. Illness is not perceived as an individual phenomenon. The element of superstition is of minor interest. In this context, the healer's task is equally to cure the patient and to redress an imbalance in the social order of the community. Almost invariably this imbalance is considered to be a result of witchcraft.

The skilled healer, through his considerable social intelligence and knowledge of the community, analyses his patient's conduct and personal relationships. The healer may agree with his patient that the illness is a machination of an enemy or the workings of the spirits. However, he is also aware of the consequences of incorrect behaviour. Has the patient failed to provide a gift of food to his parents or omitted a sacrifice at the shrine of his ancestors? Has he somehow transgressed the border of polite conduct in relation to a clansman?

Ultimately, the concern of both healer and patient is the health and sound functioning of the community; patient and community are inseparable. It is worth noting that traditional healers seem to have considerable success with certain manifestations of mental illness.[52] Usually it is the diviner, with or without the help of a herbalist healer, who determines the diagnosis by invoking the spirits. Although the treatment may include the dispensing of herbal medicines, it often takes the form of the modern concept in psychology called group therapy.

THE VALUE OF TRADITIONAL MEDICAL SERVICES

Only by considering the cultural context described above can community health become an operational and dynamic concept. Primary Health Care as a system will become operative when people assess it as a meaningful and better continuation of what they already have.

It is of major importance, therefore, to assess the value of traditional medical services. This assessment will encounter a variety of difficulties. First, there is the paucity of research in the field of traditional medicine as a result of colonial narrow-mindedness. Steps which were taken often express the bias of professionals, who lack a fundamental trust in people's ability to cope with their lives. Today, the research situation is complicated by the rapid transition of traditional societies. Sometimes, what can be observed of the activities of healers, herbalists or diviners is in a state of degeneration or decay. Methodologically, it is uncertain which research approach does justice to the subject of traditional medicine. Research questions cannot exclusively address themselves to the viability of traditional prescriptions or treatments on the basis of an origin which may be termed 'rational', i.e. derived through a process of cause and effect. Nor can the effect of a treatment be precisely measured. The ultimate yardstick of the efficacy of any health approach or programme should be the judgement of the community itself. Does it feel that the imbalance of disease and misfortune is rectified and social order restored? And the patient—does he feel that he has returned to healthy status as a community member?

Africa still provides opportunities for research in this field, but not for long. As it is, we must be satisfied with the few existing examples. Since tribal communities have survived for hundreds of years by their unique cultures, it is reasonable and probable that this indicates a successful application of unique knowledge.

POWERFUL MEDICINE

A central concept in traditional medical services is the concept of 'medicine' itself. Earlier, we noted that medicine implies everything powerful from the herbal concoction or the injection to the batteries in the transistor radio. We cannot understand this notion of medicine unless we understand the all-pervasive and powerful nature of the world of the spirits.

Almost universally, tribal societies adhere to the belief that the world is permeated by this powerful force. It inhabits inanimate matter, rock, stones, sand and soil, but is more strongly present in trees and plants and strongest in human beings. Central to this belief in a spiritual force is that it can be controlled and used by man—for good or for evil. Far from being

176

superstitious or primitive, this animism is a rational world view. It follows logically that once man acquires knowledge of these powers, he can use them in medicine with various effects. We are interested in the medicine used to promote health.

After two decades of intensive studies in traditional medicine in West Africa, Dr G.W. Harley recorded a series of interesting facts while he worked as a practitioner.[53] He observed that healers have a highly sophisticated classification system for plants and herbs with detailed information on the application of each. Particularly interesting are the prescriptions of decoctions or mixtures for common ailments such as intestinal worms, indigestion, colic and diarrhoea. The diagnoses are very detailed and specific treatments are prescribed for various types of parasites and diarrhoea. Diseases of the liver are classified into three types: (a) poisoning (or magic), (b) acute hepatitis, and (c) a chronic ailment with no cure (schistosomiasis). There are no Latin names but the different diseases were identified correctly. Whether the type of treatments prescribed would result in a high frequency of cures under controlled conditions is one consideration. More impressive is that systematic empirical methods of treatment exist for such diseases and that the community has confidence in the healer who administers the services. The traditional healer accompanies his prescription with a magical incantation of advice, as does the western doctor. The only difference is that the latter does not sing.

Genito-urinary diseases are also differentiated by the healer and are treated symptomatically. Treatment of eye ailments seems more successful. Conjunctivitis is identified and treated with an eye lotion made from a decoction of certain leaves. The inflammation is relieved at once. Sore throats are a very common ailment in Africa, as elsewhere. In terms of effective remedies, the traditional healer does not seem to be less successful than the pharmaceutical industry. Although people use a variety of wooden sticks from special shrubs as toothbrush sticks, decay is not uncommon. Elementary dental care is available. Various concoctions and pastes are used to relieve pain and stop decay. As a final remedy, a country salt (potassium hydroxide) is used, which kills the nerve. Unfortunately, it may also split the tooth.

SNAKE BITES AND IMMUNITY

An area of particular concern in tropical countries is snake bites. In terms of healing, this is often considered a speciality. Practitioners guard their knowledge as a professional secret, often through membership of secret snake societies. The use of a tourniquet is known. Part of the snake bite treatment includes sucking out the wound and making the patient vomit. It is doubtful that the various kinds of medicines used have any effect. However, the pastes applied to the wound relieve pain. Sometimes, immunization is practised by taking small doses of the venom. As always, the treatment is accompanied by intricate magic rites. For any kind of doctor the problem with snake bites is identifying the culprit among the many species in order to prescribe the correct antidote. Deaths still occur and it remains uncertain which type of doctor is the most successful.

BONE-SETTING

Bone-setting is another speciality guarded as a family secret and passed from father to son. In cases where the bone-setter's knowledge has not degenerated, the treatments seem to be uniformly successful. Traction is performed manually or with the aid of stones and ropes to secure proper alignment. Splints may then be applied. Calcine ointments and astringent pastes are used to relieve pain and aid in immobilization. Frequently, the splints are removed at intervals and massage with ointment is applied to stimulate circulation and prevent deformity.

APHRODISIACS

Aphrodisiacs and remedies against impotence and sterility constitute an area of enormous interest and activity in traditional medicine in Africa as in western medicine. We all have a craving for that kind of treatment. Need anything more be said?

SKIN DISEASES AND THE ISSUE OF CLEANLINESS

Diseases of the skin merit attention because of their implications for the general level of an individual's health. People who wear very little clothing are without protection. As a consequence, their skin is continuously exposed to insect bites, small abrasions and infections. We may have difficulty realizing the extent to which this exposure is discomforting. To remedy these daily irritants and troubles, people apply different methods. If there is access to water, they usually take frequent baths and rub their skin with soothing oil. Sometimes a kaolin base is used for an ointment of herbs which is a more permanent application. Cattlepeople such as the Galla or the Boran use a protective ointment made with a butter base. To a foreigner, the particular smells of these ointments are unfamiliar. However, it is a gross distortion for foreigners to attribute the epithet unclean to people. What foreigners are confronting is the unfamiliar. Any rural merchant of small consumer goods can testify that soap is one of his most requested items. To pronounce that people are unclean is inaccurate and immoral. It hurts to be perceived as dirty. The issue of cleanliness is exploited through paternalistic-imperialist attitudes. By branding a fellow man unclean, you exercise a control over his mind by creating a feeling of inferiority in him.

Filth is a symptom of degeneration. When it is found, it is almost exclusively in tribal cultures and villages disturbed by external influences. The traditional village is well swept and tidy. Houses are clean. Soil is deposited each morning in a new place in the bush and marked in a way that warns passers-by. Clean water supply is appreciated. If the Chaga farmer on the slopes of Kilimanjaro keeps family and cattle under the same roof, it is not due to ignorance and lack of cleanliness; it is because he is as economical and energy-conscious as his Swiss colleague who does the same.

PREVENTION IN TRADITIONAL MEDICINE

The question of skin treatment and personal hygiene leads to the question of disease prevention in traditional medicine. The notion that many diseases are contagious prevails, even though an understanding of how the disease is transferred may not be known. Isolation of sick people is often practised. Certain herbal ointments are applied to the scalp to prevent lice—and they work! Other ointments may be smeared on feet and ankles to prevent hookworm. Human faeces are almost universally surrounded by taboos, are not referred to, and are physically avoided.

The people of Lamu, an old port on an island off the coast of Kenya, knew the causal connection between static water, mosquito larvae and malaria. A plastered water-reservoir is an integral architectural feature in the anteroom of any Swahili house. Small fish were kept in the reservoir to eat the larvae, thus keeping the water clean. And what happened to the fish when the reservoir occasionally was emptied? Each reservoir has a beautiful bowl of porcelain plastered into the bottom, providing a decorative ornament and just enough water for the fish to survive until the reservoir is refilled.

MATERNAL AND CHILD HEALTH CARE

The question of prevention calls our attention to the important issues of pregnancy, antenatal care, childbirth, child care, child feeding and nutrition. Today, these areas are of central concern to Third World countries. In Africa, pregnancy is often regarded as much a spiritual as a physical reality. Considering the crucial importance of the child for the comfort of the elders and the survival of the tribal community, a pregnancy is usually accompanied by the devoted attention of the whole family. Sometimes it is considered the husband's duty to supply his wife with special foods. In Bantu societies, the institution of monogamy introduced by the missionaries contributed to the decline of the most widespread preventive measure to high child mortality—polygamy. Among the polygamous Tongas in the Zambezi Valley of Zambia, for example, it was taboo for the husband to have sexual contact with his breastfeeding wife; instead, he sent his blanket to another wife at sunset. As a child was breastfed for up to three years, and thus nurtured safely through the vulnerable age, the result of this practice was that a woman became pregnant only every second or third year. Today, under changing social conditions, she suffers from a state of continuous pregnancy and sometimes a concomitant fear of childbirth, knowing that the more frequently a woman gives birth, the greater the probability of a breech presentation and complications at delivery. Women know these consequences only too well.

MIDWIFERY

Midwifery is an institution of major concern to the rural community. Nemat Babiker, a midwife in Sudan, talked to me about the idea of introducing community health workers (CHWs). 'Problem is transport. I use donkey for travel full day and then birthing woman is dead. Camel is better for long travel. I should have camel. You ask people what they need and people say *moya* and *daya*, water and midwife. More problem is no wood for boiling water and women put refuse of cow dung on cord after I have cut. CHW can help me but will he be accepted by community?'

The seriousness of the situation is demonstrated by a conversation I had with a Sudanese nomad through an interpreter.

'Acmajid Asha's son baby is dead this morning, sir.'

'Oh, I am sorry, tell him I am sorry to hear that.'

'Acmajid Asha took camel for midwife six hours, sir.'

'Is it that far from Umkredim to El Obeid?'

'Acmajid Asha took express camel, sir, but son died and wife is very sick.'

In rural communities all over Africa the situation is similar. Aster Tessema, a woman from Welo Province in Ethiopia, revealed that she started to eat less in the third trimester of her pregnancy. She did this to prevent having a big baby, and therefore a difficult birth. I have met a similar idea among the Bemba women in Northern Province, Zambia.

What is known about traditional midwifery practices? Or rather, what is known about traditional obstetric aid? Many women have to give birth alone and aid themselves. Dr G.W. Harley reports on birth behaviour in a wide range of African tribes.[54] Although there are examples of harmful behaviour, the routine procedures are largely benign for mother and child. The problems arise from infections and abnormal presentations, although some midwives and medicine men demonstrate that they can cope even with the latter. When, for example, the traditional midwife gently shakes the patient who stands or kneels in front of her with a twisting motion from side to side and then, using all the friction she can manage, drags her hands forward over the abdomen and down towards the pubis, concluding by shaking her hand violently in front of the vulva, but not touching it, as if she wants to shake something off, she may be engaging in a symbolic procedure. At a stage of the labour when nothing of real use can be done, this procedure is probably helpful. Nor does it seem harmful towards the end of labour to administer a pinch of snuff, when it is permissible to hurry the event. A heavy sneeze helps! The cord is usually cut when the placenta has been expelled.

Various positions are adopted by women during birth. Some are reported to squat or stand in a half-crouched position holding on to a pole in front of them; some kneel on a mat supported in front by the midwife; others semi-recline in the arms of another woman. All these positions seem conducive to an easy downward birth. In no instance have I heard of women lying flat on their backs as was the custom until recently in western culture, a position which does not seem to promote birth in any sensible way. Is this routine position qualified by medical knowledge, or is it simply a cultural prejudice perpetuating a relationship of dominance, securing the subordination of the woman and the supremacy of the male medical system? We cannot always be sure where the magic tricksters really are.

CHILD FEEDING

The Tongas of Southern Africa have an expression for the placenta which reveals insights into the wonder of pregnancy and childbirth. *Yindlu ya nwana* means the house of the child. Some attention should now be devoted to child feeding, which includes breastfeeding, supplementary feeding and weaning. In subsistence societies, people generally do not sit down to meals thoughtlessly. The sharing and intake of food is a serious matter regulated by an intricate network of food taboos and norms of behaviour. The father usually eats alone or with friends; the mother eats with the children. In some tribes, complete silence is enforced; in others, *zakudya*, the big meal of the evening, is the time when stories are told and the moral code of the tribe is relayed. This does not mean that parental affection cannot be expressed by the occasional exception to the rules. As a reward for good behaviour, for example, a father may let his young son eat with him. We should also be aware that food taboos function as a mechanism for food distribution. For instance, small animals or small parts of big animals, such as the heart or the kidneys, are taboo for some age groups but not for others. Quite simply, there is not enough to share with everybody in the community. Similarly, tradition regulates the feeding of the small child: the weaning period, types of food suitable for the child, method of preparation and the manner of feeding. The whole network of rules regarding food and eating is interwoven with the social fabric of a subsistence community. This community is a delicately balanced entity in its fight for survival. We cannot alter too many rules without endangering the whole social fabric and, ultimately, the very existence of the community. For example, if a food taboo favours or reinforces the privileges of the elders, it is because the community as a whole cannot survive without access to the information possessed by the elders. With this realization, it is absurd to characterize mothers of malnourished children as ignorant. On the contrary, the mothers are often knowledgeable in the heritage of tribal information which, under normal circumstances, would be likely to secure the survival of the child. G.W. Harvey provides examples of traditional medical treatments which are essentially similar to the modern treatment of food deficiency diseases such as *marasmus* or *kwashiorkor*.[55] Malnourished children were given daily helpings of porridge made with dark-green leaves mixed with red palm-oil, substances rich in protein and vitamins. Also known was systematic exposure of small children to sunlight for the prevention of rickets.

BREASTFEEDING AND WEANING

Similarly, the rules for when and how a mother weans her child are detailed in the tribal code and have deep socio-economic implications. Nutrition educators tend to think of early weaning as a hostile act towards the child and recommend prolonged lactation. This principle is not easily applied in rural areas. The lactation period relates to the division of labour. Being responsible not only for the household chores, such as preparing food, carrying water and collecting firewood, but also for the weeding of the fields and the harvest, the woman tends to wean early in order to cope with the workload. In the urban setting, where the mother takes a full-time job, such considerations apply even more. Observers who insist that mothers breastfeed their babies in the fields have succumbed to pastoral romanticism. No mother wants to carry her child on her back when she has hard work to do. It is true that mothers can frequently be seen putting the child to the breast, but often this is for the purpose of soothing the child. The real breastfeeding takes place in the morning or the evening when the mother is rested.

The social implications of breastfeeding and child feeding are illustrated by some practical examples.

In a nutrition project in Sergipe Province in the north-east of Brazil, the objective was to improve the nutritional status of the most economically vulnerable people, the share-croppers. The strategy was to increase the share-croppers' output and then secure for them the sale of the produce at a guaranteed price. Among the women I interviewed, one alarming result of this strategy was that the husbands had loaded more work on to their wives. Subsequently, the mothers had less time to care for the children. The *flagelado*, the chastised one, the hapless peasant of Brazilian folksongs, has a hard time. But there is no doubt that his wife's lot is harder still!

From Luapula, in the Northern Province of Zambia, the men leave to seek employment in the mining towns of the Copper Belt. The women are left alone in the villages with the children and the elders. Confronted with an overwhelming workload, they have no choice but to select practices which reduce the labour in terms of time or effort. One practice is to wean the child early or bottle-feed him. Another is to switch the staple from maize to cassava. Cassava is easier to farm, gives a relatively bigger yield, and requires no seasonal effort in harvesting or storage because it can remain in the mound. The nutritional consequence of these actions has aggravated infant protein-calorie malnutrition, increased the incidence of diarrhoea and other infections from dirty feeding bottles, and reduced protein intake through the supplementary food as gruel made from cassava. Cassava has a significantly lower content of protein per unit than maize, 1 per cent to 12 per cent respectively.

These examples indicate that health and nutrition problems arise when the tribal lifestyle is in transformation or transition. It is not justified to infer that the traditional community under normal circumstances is incompetent or incapable of securing the survival of its infants. In general, there is awareness of the importance of both breastfeeding and supplementary feeding, although this information is not necessarily expressed in the terms of nutrition science.

WEANING, FIRST STEP IN SOCIALIZATION

Breastfeeding/weaning is not a mechanism which can be turned on and off when it pleases nutrition or health educators. In the first place, weaning is the primary step in the process of socialization of the child, a process of major concern to the survival of the community. It is the first occasion on which a corrective action is taken which finally leads to the child's adoption of the tribal code of behaviour. Secondly, it is a widespread notion that lactation is an impediment to cohabitation and sexual intercourse. In some societies, a man is explicitly forbidden by tribal law to cohabit with a lactating wife. In others, a woman proceeds to wean because she is pregnant again. In the context of social implications, weaning should be seen as it relates to the role of the grandparents. In Africa, it is a widespread custom to remove the weaned child to the grandparental home. As discussed earlier, this is of considerable educational importance for the child, who is often not returned to the parents' home until old enough to contribute to the family labour. If the child is very young and sulking over the emotional disengagement from his mother, it is not uncommon for the grandmother to suckle her grandchild. I have observed this on several occasions. G.W. Harley also reports extensive grandmaternal wet-nursing in Nigeria by women who have not given birth for up to 15 years.[56] This is not astonishing given the physiological fact that lactation can be stimulated. Nutrition educators who promote breastfeeding in a tribal community may well find themselves in a situation where it is more realistic to recommend wet-nursing by the grandmother than create feelings of guilt in a mother who has other pressing obligations for the survival of her family.

TRADITIONAL MEDICINE SHOULD BE RESPECTED

From the preceding, it should be recognized that diseases and malnutrition are not states of illness in individuals but community disorders which can be successfully treated only in that context. This is not a modern idea, but a fundamental principle of traditional medical services. It is interesting to note that several specific remedies now considered valuable in medical treatment, such as opium, quinine and digitalis, were not discovered by scientific research but by traditional practitioners of medicine.

Traditional doctors command a body of useful knowledge and skills that can no longer be ignored. Indeed, there is reason to subject these practices to intensive research for the community's use in the development of a relevant and appropriate primary health care function. What the traditional doctor may lack in knowledge of the physical sciences, he compensates for in his practice as community psychiatrist—a field where his work is often salutary. This does not exclude the degeneration of knowledge and the occurrence of formidable medical gangsters or small-time tricksters. Such people are found in all societies. Sincerity and pride in a profession can also be observed. And regret, when a patient fails to respond to a treatment or an adverse reaction occurs. In that respect, the traditional medical practitioner is in the same situation as the western doctor administering thalidomide who realizes belatedly that he is not an omnipotent professional, but simply a person who does his best and sometimes fails. Luckily, the World Health Organization is now promoting traditional medicine.

FOOD SURPLUS—FOOD DEFICIT

Propounders of 'economic development' seem to have overlooked the contention that improved nutrition in terms of food surplus in a subsistence society is more the cause than the consequence of social transformation. The special environmental conditions which permitted the production of a food surplus were undoubtedly the starting point for the great Egyptian civilization around the Nile basin. It is characteristic that this culture could afford to develop a written language and manifest such material enormity. The pyramids are labour-intensive monuments in stone which testify to the size and continuity of that food surplus.

It may be fruitful to regard the control of food supply—for improved food intake, for sustaining a non-food-productive labour force, and for trading—as a major determinant in establishing human material culture and economic progress.

Conversely, in this world of dichotomies, the continuous or imminent presence of a food deficit determines another type of culture. A society which barely subsists through its labour effort in food production does not release the necessary energy required for the development of elaborate material manifestations. Instead, this type of community is forced to manifest itself in a less labour-intensive and less conspicuous type of culture, the oral civilization. Being less materially conspicuous does not imply that oral civilizations are spiritually less elaborate or sophisticated. In subsistence economies, food deficit is also the determinant of social collapse and disintegration. The subsistence community survives by a fragile social formation of mutual dependence and regard among its members. Individuals know this and recognize that they cannot survive without it.

The fear of hunger, then, is not an individual's fear of the pain of the abdominal vacuum, but the communal horror of a social disaster, the extinction of the tribe. What a well-fed foreigner cannot understand is the permanence of this feeling. It is a prevailing awareness under the surface of most subsistence societies. The consciousness of this communal vulnerability accounts for the earnestness and reverence with which food is handled and referred to. The subject of food is not the source of any joke.

FOOD TABOOS AND EATING ETIQUETTE

Those who have worked in famine relief are followed for ever by the glowing eyes of the victims. In 1973, during the famine in Welo Province, Ethiopia, I met Ato Paulos Abebe, a tenant farmer from the village of Mersa. He asked me in all sincerity whether I thought he and his wife committed a sin by eating the small tin of corned beef he had just received. It was in the middle of the fast.

More than 200 days a year are, for one reason or another, declared official days of fast in Ethiopia. On those days, the taboo exclusively concerns the consumption of foods of animal origin, such as meat, milk, poultry, eggs, butter and cheese. A cooking vessel that has been in contact with any of these is considered unclean and cannot be used. On fasting days, people are allowed to eat foods only of vegetable origin, such as cereals, beans or lentils.

In subsistence societies without the same orthodox Christian or Moslem influence, food taboos and eating etiquette take other but no less rigorous forms. Broken food taboos are considered causes of disease and other disasters befalling the community. The culprit is punished. The gravity of such an offence is intensified by the fact that it is considered an insult to the ancestors and the spirits.

Groups of people are often defined by what they eat or do not eat together and by how they eat it together. For example, Hindus and Moslems have distinctly different and characteristic eating habits. Among semi-nomadic tribes such as the Maasai, Boran or Dinka, there are rules for what the various age groups can eat and how they eat it. Generally, in all tribal societies food taboos are specified for pregnant women, children and elders. Various reasons may be given for the emergence and sustenance of food taboos and eating etiquette in subsistence communities. One plausible reason seems to be the control of the limited food resources for the survival of the community. As might be expected, the concept of wealth in such societies is expressed in food terms. In Swahili, the word for prosperity, *baraka*, really means abundant harvest. And affluence, *neema*, means abundance of food.

NO 'HUNGER' BY LACK OF PROTEIN

Food deficit has some connotations which have not been sufficiently appreciated by nutritionists. Hunger, at least in the initial stages, is perceived by the individual as a feeling of emptiness. Conversely, satisfaction is the feeling of having a full stomach. In a subsistence society, the foodstuff that provides the individual with the 'feeling' of being full is the staple. *Ugali* or *nzima* (maize porridge) is eaten in sizeable portions which feel heavy, like a stone, in the stomach. No similar feeling of being full is connected with eating protein, and no hunger sensation is related to the lack of protein. This may explain why people remain malnourished for years without feeling, and consequently knowing, that they are. This circumstance poses a serious challenge for nutrition educators.

THE COMMUNITY *IS* CHANGING

The preceding paragraphs examined the constraints anticipated at the individual and the community level when trying to direct social transformation towards an improved community health status. Efforts in primary health care and nutrition aiming to promote this transformation can succeed only if the constraints are investigated, realized and accepted. A tribal community is not a collection of houses or individuals. From a functional point of view, it is a process of continuous interaction between individuals or groups of individuals who have common interests; from a structural point of view, it is a self-regulating system for the processing of information through the control of the tribal elders. This implies that social transformation comes about through a process which the community itself regulates. The community educates itself and changes its food taboos, eating habits and health-related behaviour by the force of its internal interactions. It is a common misperception that the traditional, tribal or subsistence community is conservative and resistant to change. To resist change by adhering to custom is not stupidity but wisdom. Understandably, a community does not want to abandon ideas and methods which people know and trust for new ideas untested and untried in the practical laboratory of time. Change is no newcomer to the traditional societies of Africa, which are continuously adapting and adjusting themselves with ingenuity to changing circumstances. New lifestyles emerge as a response to environmental change. New cultural manifestations flourish. Through all the changes endures the common tradition which has ensured survival, the common unity expressed in the word community.

COMMUNITY CONSENSUS

Social transformation in modern Africa will not take an appropriate direction unless the traditional African community is better understood. A social transformation, by definition, is something which can happen only to a social formation. If genuine change is desired, it will occur only through the social mechanisms for change which the community has established and to which it is accustomed. People are eager to change behaviour if they perceive the change as beneficial. The change is set in motion through the mechanism of *community consensus.* The consensus is sometimes overt, sometimes tacit. The way it is achieved may vary with the community's social organization or structure. The community is a self-regulating social formation that processes information. It will decode, select or reject incoming information and compare it with information stored in its memory. Ultimately, the community will produce new information accepted or regarded as normative for individual behaviour and conducive to the communal interest.

Significant research experiences have accumulated on the smallest type of social formation, the group. This applies particularly to extension work in health and nutrition. Regarding food and the eating habits of adults, behaviour change through the passive approach of extension talk or lecture with or without visual aids is significantly less effective than a group dynamic approach where the group discusses the issue and arrives at a consensus of decision and action.[57] Education in the nutrition rehabilitation of malnourished children in Uganda, a process of group interaction where mothers who had rehabilitated their babies demonstrated the dietary cure to mothers with sick children, was significantly more effective than talks to the mothers by nutrition educators.[58]

THE ELDERS AGAIN

With good reason, group interaction and consensus in daily life are, by a long tradition, the mechanisms used by the village community to process information and to make decisions. The system persists because it works—and with a minimum of conflict. With reference to the earlier analysis of the role of the elders in processing information in the community, we realize that the elders' position in the system is critical to its function. In any system for information processing, the principle is the stepwise advancement of the impulses through 'gates', which let them through or stop them. The elders function as gatekeepers as well as the memory of the process. One primary purpose of the elders is to minimize conflict in order to preserve the community as a functioning, surviving unit. Conflict is minimized and functionality maximized if the information has the features of identifiability, recognizability, familiarity and acceptability.

This analysis emphasizes the need to include the elders when a project requiring social transformation is introduced in the community. New information should be conceptualized in forms familiar and appropriate to people's ways of expression. Proverbs, riddles, tales, or whatever form is customary should be adopted and adapted as the means of communication. It is easier for a village community to turn its eyes to the future if it starts by looking at its past. I have never encountered a community which is not interested in the history of the tribe and the ways of the ancestors. How did people do it in the old days? Why did they do it like that? What are we doing now? Why are we doing it like this? What is the situation to-day? How can we do it better? When people become aware of the changes they have experienced, the prospect of new change becomes more meaningful and acceptable.

It is essential and urgent to realize that deprecatory statements about traditional ways of life and denouncements of people's customs are counterproductive in any process of social transformation. Traditional values should be recognized and appreciated for their special contribution to a better future.

MINIMAL ACCESS TO MODERN MEDICAL SERVICES

This brings us to the question of the potential contribution of the traditional medical services to the health of the community. The statistics on modern medical staff in some African and European countries reveal a striking picture.[59]

Population per doctor, medical assistant, nurse or pharmacy

Country	Doctor	Med. ass.	Nurse	Pharmacy
Angola	15,170	15,060	1,870	66,800
Ethiopia	84,350	134,010	25,670	896,190
Kenya	11,420	14,470	1,070	73,600
Tanzania	18,490	24,350	3,300	409,280
Nigeria	14,810		3,210	42,460
Zaire	27,950	245,810	11,700	174,500
United Kingdom	760		270	3,510
Sweden	580		120	2,130

Although some African countries have made considerable progress and although there may be discrepancies in the staff categories, this table reveals clearly that only a fraction of the population has access to modern medical care. It is no secret that this fraction is the élite, usually housed in the urban areas. The fact is that *the overwhelming majority of the population survives with the aid of traditional doctors.* Most people do not have access to alternative services. Given the reality that the growth in medical personnel is outstripped by the population growth, rural people will not be provided with alternative services for many generations. It is incomprehensible—and a waste of valuable human resources—that national governments and international organizations in the field of health care and nutrition continue to plan and act as if traditional medical service do not exist. The major practical problem is the upgrading of these services.

NATIONAL EXTENSION SERVICES

Communities are not completely isolated social formations. They exist in a larger social context. In that context, national governments are a fact of life, however faint their influence in the daily affairs of the local community. In a process of nationally directed social transformation, drastic structural change by various revolutionary means may be advocated as a necessity in many countries, for example forms of decentralized communally structured activities. However, man is not yet capable of taking into use social formations which can function without centralized organizational frameworks in one form or another. Such frameworks are vestiges of social control. They are generally considered the means through which government, political parties and people should express themselves. As intimated in earlier chapters, doubt can justifiably be raised about such notions. They stand for a type of social formation which tends to obstruct the creative flow of information, to create authority without order, and to lead to the formation of vested interests and, ultimately, the exploitation of people.

Most national governments have extension services in agriculture, health, adult education, community development, and other fields. In health, the extension services are part of the infrastructure of modern medical services. However small their general impact is on the local community's health status, these services seem indispensable in certain areas.

EPIDEMIOLOGICAL DISEASES

In epidemiological diseases, causal relationships are complex and outside the conceptual framework of the traditional doctor. It is estimated that approximately one thousand million people risk malaria in the poverty belts of the world.[60] River-blindness, which drives people out of some food productive areas, is estimated to affect 20 million people in Africa. Sleeping sickness, which limits livestock grazing, afflicts 35 million. Schistosomiasis, also connected with food productive areas, is estimated to affect between 180 and 200 million people. Disaster relief for these people is provided through national governments, with extensive aid from the international community. To a large extent, the success of disaster relief will depend on the availability and degree of efficiency of the national infrastructure in providing modern medical services. The health extension services make up one of the few tenuous links with some local communities.

ADMINISTRATIVE SOLUTIONS

By virtue of their nature as civil service organizations, conventional public health services tend to occupy themselves with health problems that can be solved administratively. Campaigns for eradication of malaria, smallpox, etc. become problems of logistics and management. Administering vaccinations to hundreds of persons a day is an exhausting task. Knowledge and application of general social communication methods or methods in health and nutrition education play little, if any, role in the daily work of the health extension worker. For example, knowledge of the group consensus approach would not exist, nor would there be time to use it, if it did exist. Staff in local clinics or dispensaries and in health education and extension services work against odds seldom realized. Now, with the need for introducing primary health care (PHC), it is of the utmost importance to examine the situation.

HEALTH WORKER OPINIONS

Below are verbatim statements in English from interviews I had with a group of health workers in an African country. I feel that the statements provide useful insights into the difficulties the health workers encountered, the attitudes they developed and the opinions they held, particularly in connection with the planned mass introduction of health extension workers with a minimal requirement in formal education—the community health workers (CHWs).

Fatima (nurse): Prevention is better than cure. We have to thank PHC to give us the chance of preventing in our own people. We do too much theoretical action. Our people do not believe us. People build clinic house, but government do not fulfil promise so people do no self-help again. We are the military people in health education. We are willing to go and die to change people's bad health habits.

Zahraa (nurse and teacher of CHWs): PHC is very important for happiness of people and will be successful if CHW can go into every house, but selection not proper. Village headman often put in relative. Tutoring started without tutors being in good picture about the programme PHC and books lack for tutoring.

Mohammad (medical assistant): For nomads CHW should know more camel diseases and sickness of cattle. Nomads know diagnosis through smell of stools, but not isolation of sick animals during movements. Without camel nomad die even he has no sickness himself. Biggest problem is nomad return to village. Headman own well. People fight for water. My treatment is all time wounds of knife.

Sheraf (medical assistant): Health education at social events of burials and weddings are no good. People are disturbed. I call meeting at appropriate time through *el monadi*—the town crier, that is. I get support of elders for health education, then I lecture people about their wrong habits and diseases.

Bashir (medical assistant): I am medical assistant with good paper. CHW have not same paper. Some are small—15-16 years. Even if they have school before they are too small for going unsupervised due to the mountains in my district.

In conclusion, the opinion of a medical doctor also present in the group.

Dr Firmo: The first aim of health education should be to health educate our civil servants and politicians so that they understand PHC. Then, we need more clinics and dressing stations. Within five miles radius attendance is high, beyond ten miles statistics show attendance is zero. People do not walk that far. And we need more space: the patient does not get rest because of all the visitors. It is as if five or six extra people are admitted with the patient. The hospital ward looks like a market place. Even the football team is coming to hospital if a player is hurt.

The complexities of the field situation are seldom profoundly understood at the administrative centre of the public health services. There is an enormous discrepancy between the ideas, strategies and plans developed at the centre and their implementation in the field. Conventional health education can be said to operate as if reality did not exist. The contention that health education does not work may be true—but then, the reason is that it has never really been tried.

THE PROFESSIONAL BANKRUPTCY OF NATIONAL HEALTH SERVICES

To understand what is happening, let us look at national public health services including health and nutrition education as social formations which process information. In this system, the flow of information is constantly interrupted, distorted and blocked by conflicts of interests and counterproductive ideas and attitudes deriving from élitism, vested interests and class distinctions.

Here are some of the simple obstructing phenomena which can be observed in almost any health establishment.

The staff belong to the educated élite. Therefore, typical bourgeois values permeate the hierarchy from the top to the level of the fieldworker. Reality is seen through the reports of the latter, who knows his superiors only welcome 'facts' which are consistent with their social values and views. Large amounts of pseudo-information are concentrated around the false fact that poverty and ill health are caused by ignorance. This allows the establishment to launch masses of educational programmes, the purpose and result of which only distract attention from the need for a structural change in society and a redistribution of wealth. In the process, the livelihood of the health education establishment is sustained.

Health and nutrition messages processed by the system have been devised and meted out according to the measure stick of the middle-class bureaucrat behind a desk. With their frequent characterizations of rural or village people's actions as mistakes, habits as bad and attitudes as wrong, they reflect a feudalistic lack of trust in the ability of common people to cope with their lives.

Through the application of professional jargon, the programmes are given a pseudo-scientific coating which deceives the boards of the international funding agencies into support. Collection of baseline data is propounded and the need for evaluation is advocated, but the self-searching attitude which is the basis for determining realistic statements or conclusions is not there. Is there no good will and no sincere attempt at analysis and programme formulation for the betterment of people's lives? Of course there is, but progress in this area depends on our ability to identify and expose a type of organizational behaviour which impedes it. We need more knowledge about mechanisms of domination. There is little doubt that the pattern of working life in an organizational bureaucracy of which health services are a part retards emerging moves towards change.

Enthusiastic and perceptive community health workers can be given training and made to realize through self-experience the importance of new ideas and approaches. However, the problem remains that sensitive field workers are quickly overwhelmed by the system and lapse into fulfilling its expectations upon return to their work milieu.

'Health for all', the slogan used by the primary health care movement, is considered a hope by many. It is an enigma that some consider the slogan a threat.

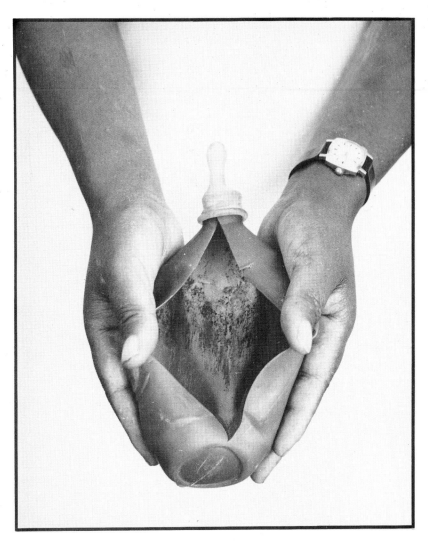

One lethal example of modernization is the feeding bottle. These are baby killers, particularly when like this one they are not transparent. The mother cannot see the dirt, much less clean it, because the neck is so narrow. Local plastics factories which manufacture colourful washtubs, foodbowls, plates and feeding bottles provide employment and governments are reluctant to interfere with their production and marketing. Feeding bottles should have an approved design and be available only on prescription. The government of Papua New Guinea is one of the few Third World governments which has introduced a law regulating the marketing of feeding bottles.

Members of the Bemba tribe in Zambia leave the object which the deceased cherished most in life on the grave. The object may be an old stool, a hat, a walking stick, or anything else. In 1968, in a graveyard in Lusaka, I found dozens of graves like this one. The new food industry in Third World countries which markets milk powder and baby foods to unsuspecting consumers is committing mass infanticide in the name of economic development.

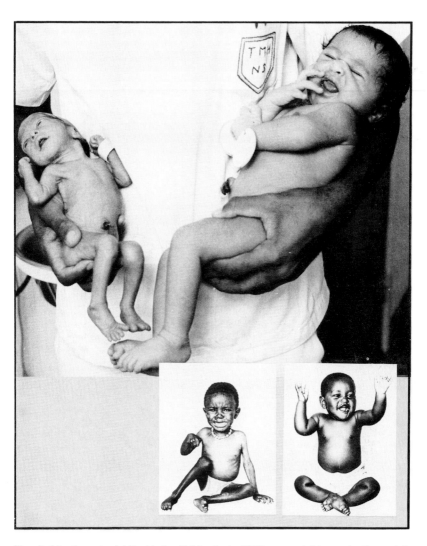

Two babies born in Addis Ababa, Ethiopia, in 1973, one weighing only 1kg and the other the normal 3.5kg. The single most important factor in the excessive perinatal and infant mortality rates in Third World countries is the high percentage of babies with low birth weight due to socio-economic deprivation.[61] Low birth weight is a handicap for life. Economic growth factors are false indicators of socio-economic development. Social transformation towards a better quality of life for all through improved nutrition and primary health care can be measured by positive health indices, such as birth-weight distribution and nutritional status.

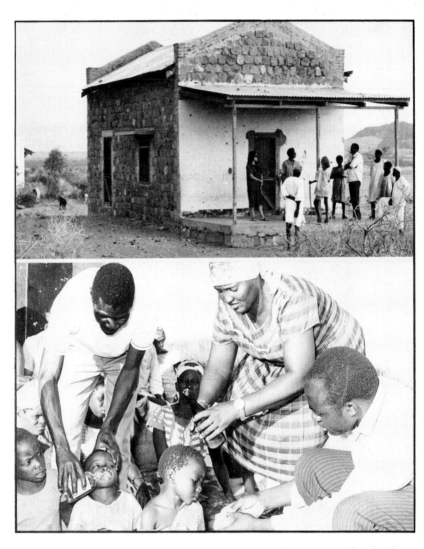

An empty health clinic near Unkredim, Sudan. For the last two months, the clinic had been without a nurse. Generally, rural health clinics play an insignificant role in people's lives. The community willingly provides the housing, but the government often does not have the managerial capacity to honour its promises. Consequently, the supply of staff and drugs is either sporadic or non-existent.

Even in urban areas people still rely mainly on the traditional medical practitioners, some of whom are quick to exploit the opportunity. This woman practised her skills in a township outside Lusaka, Zambia.

It is an élitist myth that village people are conservative and unwilling to try new ideas. On the contrary, they adapt quickly to new ways and adopt new technology if they need it. The 'debe', a tin can usually holding four gallons of liquid, was used to import oil and kerosene to East Africa. Once the empties became available in large quantities, people converted them into containers for transporting water. The standardized size and nationwide availability quickly established the tin container as a fixed measure. Now, sweet potatoes, onions and maize flour are bought by the 'debe' in the markets.

This small kerosene lamp is one of many examples of efficient recycling and adaptation of introduced technology to local needs at a locally reasonable cost.

13
pictures by people

'What do you see in this picture, Mulilo?'
Mulilo: *'I see motoka.'*
'Have you seen many motorcars here in Mfue?'
Mulilo: *'I have seen . . . I have seen in my head.'*

PICTURE AND MEMORY-PICTURE

A potter or a woodcarver in a village community in Africa knows, in a sense, more about pictures than a modern photographer. We need to realize a very simple thing. Village people gain their knowledge through handling, creating or looking at objects and events. Therefore, when people see pictures, they expect the pictures to contain what they *know* about the objects—not only what they *see* of the objects. My impression is that people carry in their heads very vivid and intense memory-pictures. These memory-pictures are more realistic to them than a flat picture on a piece of paper. The memory-picture comprises 'pictures' of an object from various angles as the object is perceived in a person's daily involvement with it. There is a discrepancy between the photograph of a man in which only one leg and one arm are visible and the memory-picture of a man or the gestalt of a man. The gestalt is the memory of the whole man who comprises a body with front, back and sides, two legs, two arms, and a face with two eyes, two ears, a nose and a mouth.

DRAW ME A LORRY!

During filming on location in a fairly remote village in the Eastern Province of Zambia, we were accommodated in a school classroom. I happened to ask one of the older pupils to draw me a lorry on the blackboard. A couple of old lorries were regularly in the area. The drawing was a long process with the student biting his lip and giving an occasional sigh. Upon reaching the stage shown in illustration A, he apparently experienced a crisis. He hesitated, retreated a step, and contemplated the drawing. Suddenly, he seemed to have overcome his problem, completing the picture in one go as in illustration B. He brushed the chalk off his hands and turned to me with an air of having accomplished his task.

We must envisage that the memory-picture is dynamic. As time passes, it becomes more and more structured for the perceiving subject.

A   B

Insignificant details vanish and significant details assume a stronger position. The memory-picture becomes a gestalt in which the details have valence in relation to the whole according to their visual and emotional connotation for the person. A memory-picture is more concrete to the person than the two-dimensional picture on paper which is more abstract. A lorry has a clear, concrete visual gestalt characterized by the high valence of the four wheels. For a person who experiences his inner picture with concrete qualities, it is logical and meaningful to make all four wheels visible. There is no clear distinction between the real and the apparent, between the memory-picture and the here-and-now visual impression.

FROM ANTIQUITY TO FUNCTIONALITY

The memory-picture is exactly what we witness in artistic expressions from ancient cultures. The following series of pictures show that artists from antiquity 'twisted' objects in space. They drew what they knew about objects rather than what they actually saw in front of them. In other words, artists saw objects through their experience. They projected a visual gestalt into a two-dimensional reality. If village people found it useful or necessary to make pictures, probably they would paint them in a similar manner. Pictures made by people reflect what people know in a concrete way. Although they would not use the word, people know that what they see of an object from a certain angle in a single moment is 'the abstraction of the moment'. In an oral culture, people deal efficiently with perception through the ear. Pictorial perception through the eye is less developed and must be learned. To facilitate the process of learning and to be of use in a process of community discussion, pictorial material should be adapted to the visual limits of the village community. This implies an adjustment to the figure/background phenomenon and an attempt to encourage people to act the themes of the pictures themselves. The process of acting directs people's attention towards the theme of what they are doing which, invariably, *is* the community issue. Acting out the picture reinforces the picture as a meaningful experience in itself. The photographer's role is as an instrument in the production of the picture. On the following pages are examples of attempts to apply these criteria in practice.

To the pictorially trained eye, a health education aid in the visual environment of the village would look something like A. To the untrained eye (B), the contrasts may be more striking, but many details remain unstructured in the perception. The purpose of a graphic layout is to permit the viewer to structure the whole by helping him/her to see the significant details.

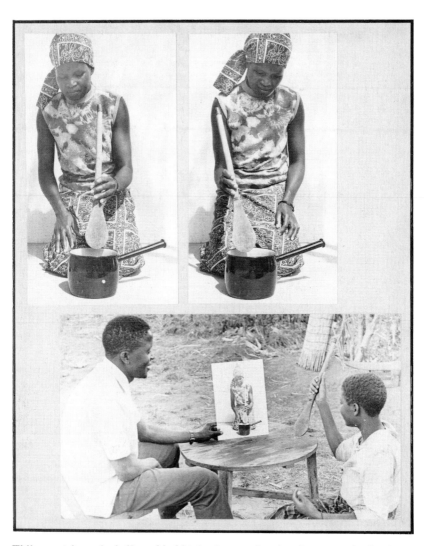

Will you pick up the ladle and hold it in the same hand as the woman in the picture. Sixty-five per cent of 68 rural women from Western Province, Zambia, chose the wrong hand in relation to the picture. The ability to imagine oneself turned round 180 degrees in space is a skill of abstraction which takes some time to acquire. We should be aware that the untrained eye may initially perceive pictorial representations more as objects than as pictures of objects.

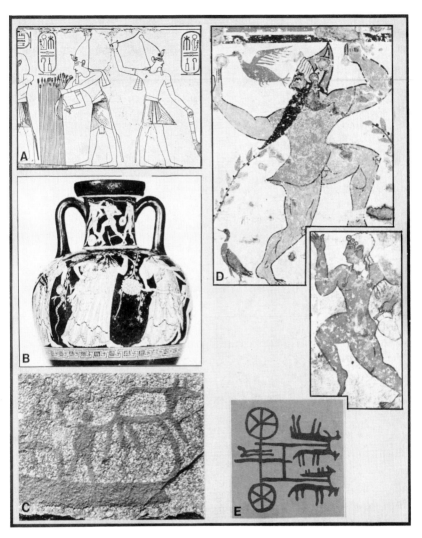

When people do not make a clear distinction between the real and the apparent, they twist the objects in space and paint what they see with their experience. A. A relief from Medinat Habu featuring Pharaoh Rameses III reaping his harvest, 1200BC. B. A classic antique vase dating from 500BC. C. A Scandinavian rock carving, thousands of years BC. D. Two wall paintings from the tombs of the Lionesses at Tarquinia, Etruria, 530BC. E. An antique chariot rock carving found in the Libyan Desert. All display the twisted style which continued up to the Renaissance in AD1400, when perspective was introduced in painting.

The naturalistic, mechanical camera-eye picture is a simplistic, incomplete reproduction of the object. A twisted 'memory-picture' is far superior because it communicates more information about the object. Visual aids should be optimally functional in relation to people's perceptual habits, but solutions such as these may be technically difficult to achieve.

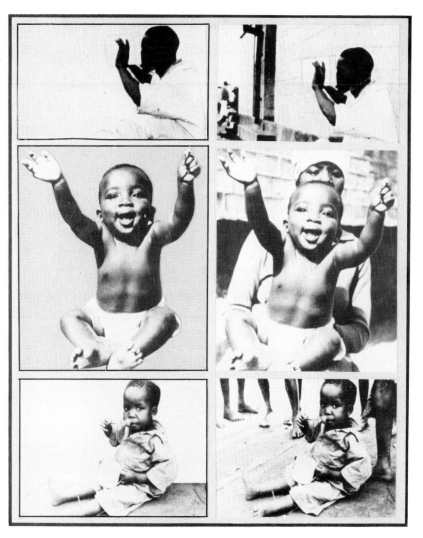

Elimination/concentration is a fundamental principle which should be applied in the layout of all visual aids. These three pairs of pictures are self-explanatory.

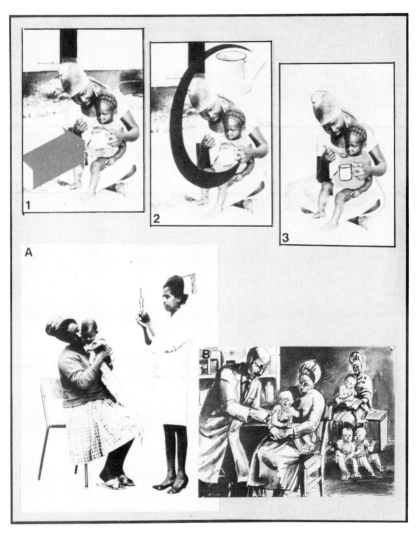

These three different layouts for a visual aid on cup and spoon feeding of children illustrate the kind of solution often found in practice. But does the arrow point? Does the curve combine the details? Not unless people have learned to read the cue. Perhaps the third solution is closest to the essential message. In the two examples showing vaccination, people had great difficulty seeing what was happening in picture B, whereas A—in which the figure/background principle was used—was easily understood.

A. Some countries, such as Ethiopia, have a strong pictorial tradition full of national character which could be utilized in visual aids. This handout in Amharic is on breastfeeding and supplementary food. B. People are fascinated when they identify illustrations of their own proverbs and stories. It is like solving riddles: 'One cannot climb two trees at a time, even if one has two feet.' C. 'Knowledge that is not expressed is like a lamp in a clay pot.' D. 'Given time, the egg starts to walk.'

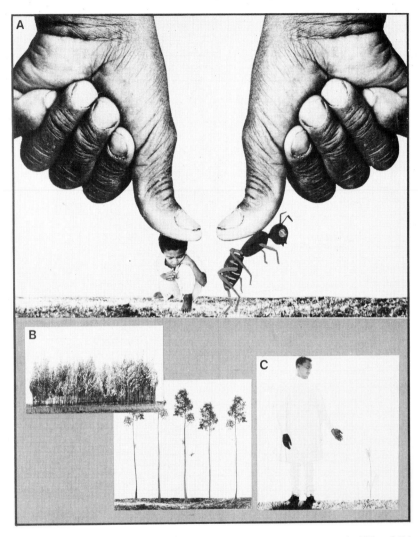

A. A health campaign for better child care can well utilize this proverb: 'The child and the ant are always made to suffer.' B. The concept of child spacing can be conspicuously demonstrated in a country where people know the economics of eucalyptus trees. C. Man is huge compared to the grain.

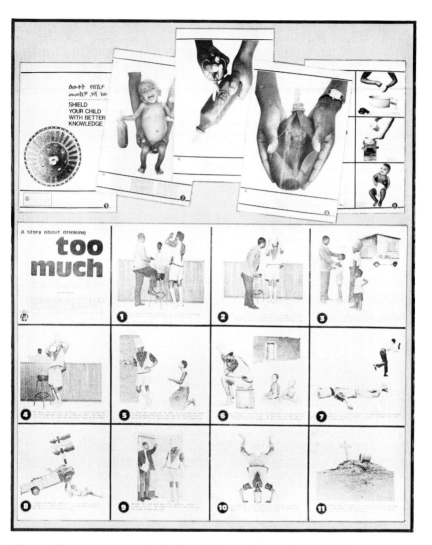

From a flip-over series on the feeding bottle and a story about drinking too much. Beer drinking is closely associated with malnutrition. People are willing actors in this wall-cartoon demonstrating the typical disastrous consequences. It is the experience that those who can read are reading for those who cannot.

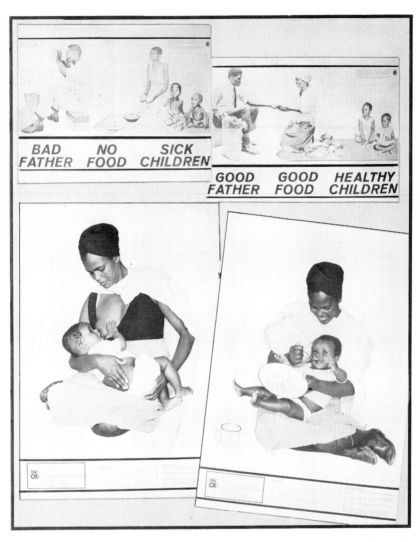

BAD NO SICK
FATHER FOOD CHILDREN

GOOD GOOD HEALTHY
FATHER FOOD CHILDREN

Another series on beer drinking and malnutrition. Value judgements about the father are sometimes necessary when the mother and the children suffer. These two charts are 'instant stories' comprising in a natural way a series of details and events. When tested in rural areas, 80 per cent of the respondents identified the message without the text.

Breastfeeding and supplementary feeding are crucial factors in reducing child mortality.

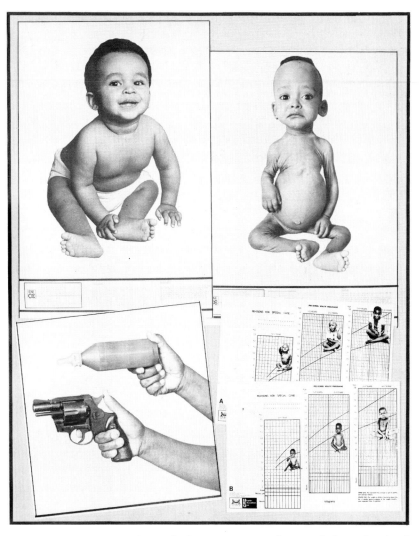

When most babies are malnourished, it is important that people form the visual concept of 'a healthy baby'.

The plastic feeding bottle is a baby killer. It is sometimes necessary to dramatize this fact.

Doctors try to establish the concept of growth by plotting the baby's weight on a chart, but teaching such an abstraction is difficult.

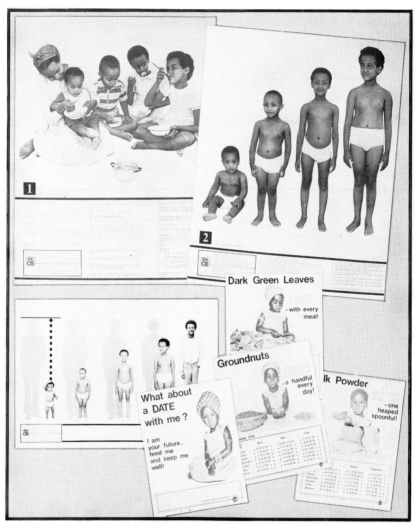

Three charts on the connection between food and growth for communities with different levels of reading skills. The charts also have guideline texts for the field worker.

Calendars are coveted items in women's clubs, health clinics, local government offices and classrooms.

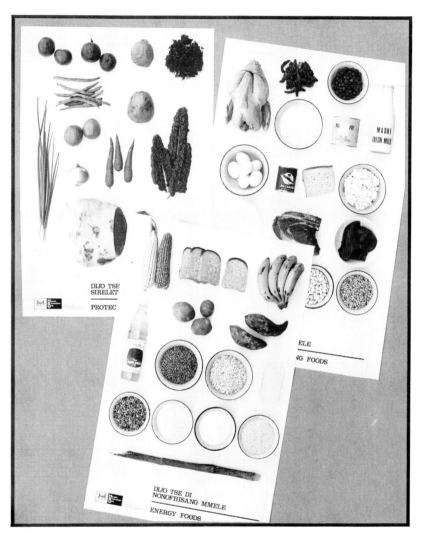

Foods should be reproduced as they really are, preferably in colour and at the angle at which they are usually seen. Too many education aids in nutrition are unintelligible.

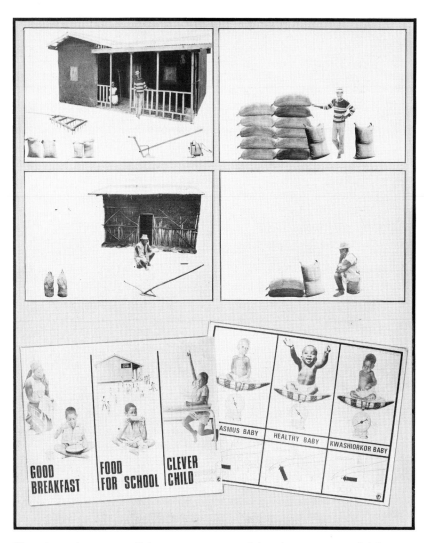

Two charts from a parallel series on a successful and not so successful farmer.

Hungry and therefore inattentive students are a common phenomenon in rural schools. Because this chart clearly combines the elements of the story, people found it easy to understand without the text.

Another effort in trying to explain the weight chart.

We asked Belainesh to show us how she keeps her baby clean and healthy. She acted the story used in this flip-over series. Note that each chart has an explanatory text giving the cue to the 'storyteller' and preparing her for the questions likely to be asked.

215

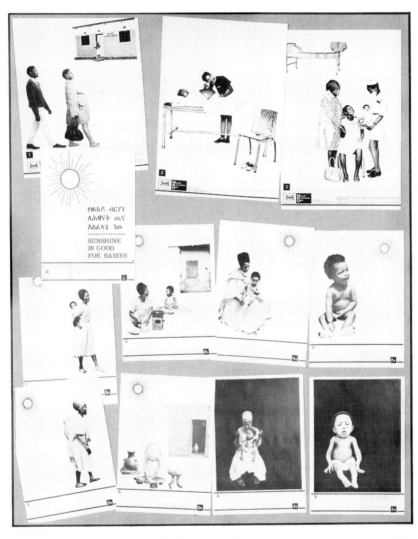

Clinics are not always accessible, but when they are regular check-ups and delivery at the clinic are best and safest.

In some countries, rickets is a major problem. These two mothers each have a different story to tell. The field worker should let people work out the stories themselves by looking at the pictures.

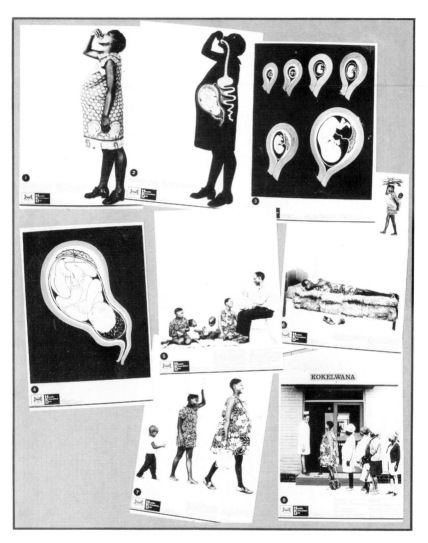

Antenatal care, adequate nutrution, rest, help from family members and regular check-ups are important health issues in Botswana, as anywhere else.

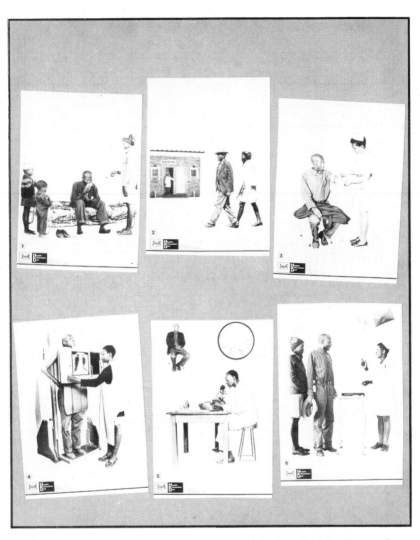

On this page and the next: Cure and prevention of tuberculosis is a long and complex story. Mr Nwako, who had survived the disease, acted it out willingly with his family.

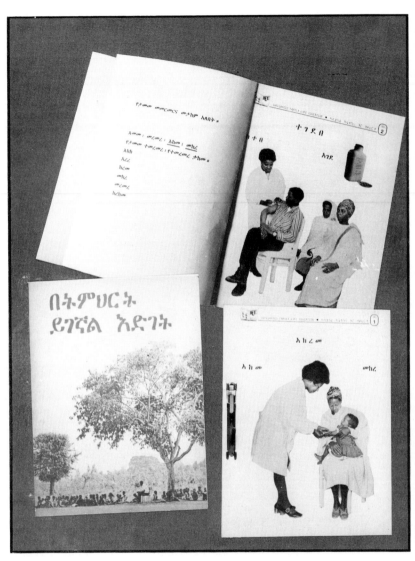

Literacy reader in Amharic produced for an adult education programme in Ethiopia. The reader is based on the principle that students are given a cover and one sheet at a time to be inserted into it. Lessons begin with community concepts such as vaccination or the correct use of medication. People acted out the situations in the pictures.

Despite the lip-service paid to maternal and child health care, these areas receive very low priority in governmental budgets.

What can we do to convince the decision-makers? The child is a development issue.

14
tenderness towards things

*' The committee's investigators found
higher than permissible levels of
radioactivity in several swimming pools,
in the urine of nearby residents and even
in the chocolate cake baked in the Tucson
public school's central kitchen.'*
Newsweek, *July 9th, 1979*

IS THERE ANY ABSOLUTION?

It has never been quite clear to me why human beings should be the great-
est and most impressive of all animals. Occasionally, I have encountered
dolphins. They don't kill each other. They live submerged in total harmony with their environment, enjoy a peaceful, stable community life and
possess a seemingly sustained sense of humour.

'This land is mine,' said the colonizer. 'We belong to the land,' answered the people born and bred on it. The mellow peoples of Papua New
Guinea, who speak Pidgin-English, would say: 'Land bilong yu mi'—and
maybe that's the way it is.

What of the life on the land? For some time, we have regarded fishing
and hunting as hostile acts towards other creatures. And let us not talk of
the murdering of human beings. Only recently have we come to acknowledge our large-scale theft from the environment. The reason why we continue to feel more superior than guilty is our invention of a psychological
survival device called absolution.

ANIMALS, PLANTS AND THINGS ARE CLOSE RELATIVES

When the North American Indian or the African tribesman refers to the
eagle or the bear, the tortoise or the leopard as their totem, we dismiss it as
superstition or regard it with amused generosity. We do not understand
that people identify these animals as their brothers and sisters. This is a
very advanced ethic. What a lovely thought that animals and plants and
other things in our environment are close relatives. Look at the small
stones sitting along the path we walk. I can sit like a stone, quite still for a
long while with my eyes closed and see many images inside me. Yes, the
stones have spirits inside them also . . .

WE SHOULD APOLOGIZE

We are dismembering the animals, slashing the trees, grinding the fruits, smashing the stones. We should apologize; we are dismembering the spirits. Some people do offer an apology. These are the BaMbuti, small people of the Ituri Forest in Zaire, and the !Kung San, small people of the Kalahari Desert in Botswana.[62] In 1980, these people believe man should be grateful for the abundance of his environment. If you must kill an animal for food, the least you can do is say a prayer to the spirit of the animal apologizing for the act. Some people still display tenderness towards things.

THE HUNTER-GATHERERS

Despite their widely differing environments, the BaMbuti and the !Kung San share an important feature, they are hunter-gatherers. They do not live in permanent settlements, do not grow crops or keep cattle. These people are moving constantly in quest of food, hunting small or bigger animals, gathering fruits, plants, berries, honey and insects. One of the most striking characteristics of these people is their tenderness in social relationships, their politeness, their enjoyment of socializing. The reader should not be tempted to think that I am advocating a return to a naturalist/romanticist view of paradise on earth. From the viewpoint of the social sciences, we should be particularly concerned about the few hunting-gathering societies that remain. People settled as agriculturalists only 10,000 years ago. This event had unquestioned significance for the evolution of society. As discussed previously, it led to social formations which produced a food surplus, thereby sustaining a labour force with various skills. The development of these skills precipitated the evolution of material cultures. As the population of the earth becomes urban, this process accelerates. By the turn of this century, most people will be living in cities.

1.5 MILLION YEARS AS A HUNTER-GATHERER

In terms of mankind's history, 10,000 years of development is microscopic. Preceding it is the enormous expanse of approximately 1.5 million years. During this period, man survived as a hunter-gatherer, first as *homo erectus* and later as *homo sapiens*. Before that, *homo habilis*, not quite so astute, spent another 1.5 million years developing his brain, shaping his teeth and producing the first simple tools. In our history, the epoch of unquestionable significance in shaping modern man both physically and mentally was that of the hunter-gatherer. We stand to learn more about ourselves—and perhaps intimations about our future—by studying the hunter-gatherers social organization, their behavioural code, their relationship to the environment, and their ways of communication with the spirits.

OPEN AND FLEXIBLE SOCIAL FORMATIONS

One of the most interesting features of hunting-gathering people is the nature of their social organization, although that expression is inadequate. No hierarchical structures or centralized authority figures exist. On the contrary, it seems that every effort is directed to prevent such structures developing. The hunter-gatherers live and work in open, flexible social formations, bands of 20 to 30 people moving over a certain territory in cycles according to the seasons. And there is no territorial imperative. If, for example, there is an abundance of fruit in a particular location, neighbouring bands are welcome. Generally, the size of the territory is related to the size of the band it sustains. Hunting and gathering is not a haphazard roaming of a territory, picking or shooting whatever is found. Rather, it is a systematic activity. People know with great accuracy where to go to find what at which time of the year. They *know* their territory and the life it supports. Intimate knowledge of animal behaviour is part of any hunter's weaponry.

RESTRUCTURING OF THE FORMATIONS

At different times of the year, all the bands gather for seasonal events by water holes or for hunts. These gatherings offer opportunities for socialization in a wider context than the band. Celebrations and feasts, initiation ceremonies and weddings take place. At these gatherings, a restructuring of the social formations seems to occur and the composition of the bands is often altered before they set out again. A family may decide to leave one band and join another, perhaps because they like a certain family in that band. A sponger may realize that his time is up. A braggart may look for another audience. If two men have had a confrontation, they do not hunt together the next time; quarrels are solved by separating the quarrellers. Through the simple device of frequent reshuffling of individuals among the bands, social tension in the tribe as a whole is diffused and conflict in the bands is minimized. The tribe functions in the context of a structure, but not a hierarchical one. This reshuffling mechanism, which operates more or less tacitly, is similar to some practices in today's management methods. In terms of information processing, this mechanism maximizes the utilization of the information resources of the tribe by continuously recombining these resources. Kinship is the tie creating overall coherence in the tribe and its bands.

AN ANALYTIC BRAIN

For hunter-gatherers, sophisticated technology and ornate material culture are dysfunctional. This is why they do not develop them. Their culture is highly oral and mental, or should we say spiritual. Hunter-gatherers are proficient in their particular vocation. Stalking an animal through the bush demands as much intellectual skill as physical stamina.

Only an integrated analysis of a multitude of factors, from the age of the animal tracks to wind direction, and knowledge of an animal's habits can secure success and survival. The gathering of fruit also requires an intricate factor analysis. To minimize labour input and maximize result, it is necessary to know precisely when the fruit is ripe, in which location, under what weather conditions, and at what time of the year. Our brain probably developed significantly during this 1.5 million year long pursuit.

DIVISION OF LABOUR

Another significant social feature in hunting-gathering societies is the nature of the division of labour. Men hunt for the meat and women gather edible greens, fruit and nuts. Approximately two-thirds of a hunter-gatherer's diet consists of the latter. Woman's role in mankind's development seems to have been grossly underestimated. In a sense, she has experienced unwitting discrimination by archaeology. Male technology, the hand axes and choppers in stone, survived the ravages of time. However, female technology, the basket and the digging stick made of perishable materials such as animal skin, plant fibres or wood, did not survive. Over thousands of years, symbolism centred around the male implements, the axe, knife or sword in stone or metal. A masculine image came to dominate the perception of our past because a few objects were hardier than others. As it appears today, the baskets and the digging sticks which perished probably held deeper significance for the development of society.

THE BASKET AND THE INVENTION OF 'SHARING'

Whereas hunting was an exciting, challenging and high-risk venture which often failed, gathering formed the group's socio-economic base. Labour investment in gathering gave a high and predictable rate of return. When the woman invented the basket, it led to a technological leap forward comparable to the invention of the wheel. With the basket, a degree of delayed consumption became possible and the uniquely human characteristic of *sharing* probably developed. The woman could travel further away from the camp collecting sizeable quantities of roots, fruits, shoots, eggs and other edibles in the basket. With the basket on her back, or by her side, the woman achieved greater mobility. She could now carry not only food but also her child. On return, the abundance of the basket was there to share with others, next-of-kin and friends. Eating advanced from individual consumption from the trees to a social event, the meal. Through the advent of sharing emerged uniquely human attitudes. We all recognize the emotional loading of such concepts as generosity, hospitality, lavishness, stinginess, reciprocity, obligation or responsibility. From sharing evolved the notion of the gift, and much later the idea of altruism. The function of sharing and cooperation was fundamental to the survival of the hunting and gathering society. With limited technology, hunting was by necessity a coordinated strategy executed by a group of hunters in collaboration—although circumstance would occasionally allow the clever hunter to feature as an individual hero. However, the premise of the obligation to share was the social mechanism through which the hunting-gathering societies retained their fundamental egalitarianism.

SHARING WITH OTHER CREATURES

Survival through sharing seems to have another significance. A band of hunter-gatherers generally uses the food resources of its territory below its capacity. This appears to be the expression of a pragmatic attitude based on securing an availability of food for the future. Hunter-gatherers are guided by a deep-rooted ethical attitude to their environment: nature's abundance is to share with other creatures and the spirits. This egalitarian principle is expanded beyond human society to encompass man's relationship to other animals and nature as a whole. We, the ravaging exploiters of nature, dare call this primitivism? Ultimately, what matters most in and *for* our lives is our attitudes. In this pervasive sharing attitude of the hunter-gatherers, we can acknowledge the great human resource of sensitivity and tenderness. We can do this without regressing to romanticism.

UNITY IN DIVERSITY

The marvel of Africa is its expressive diversity—from the Tuaregs, the Berbers and the Arabs of the North to the Lozi, the Shona and the Zulu of the South; from the Amharas, the Anuaks, the Maasai and the Swahili of the East to the Ashanti, the Yoloff and the Yoruba of the West, and many others. Africa is a sparkling multitude of peoples seasoned in the fight for survival and in the art of living. Because it comprises desert, savannah, rain forest, mountain, lake, river and ocean and because it suffers so many natural disasters—drought, flood and storm—Africa also demonstrates a variety of social responses to environmental challenges. Although social formations have emerged in sophistication and splendour, the majority are characterized by a functional simplicity. Africa offers unique examples of social behaviour from which western society has much to learn. Our sociologists have gone astray. They analyse man's behaviour in western society as if only one social model is thinkable and desirable. Africa demonstrates a variety of social models, some of which provide viable options for a restructuring of western society in a more humane direction.

Far from being anachronisms, tribal societies in Africa are pools of valuable social experience and sociological knowledge which the world should record before they are destroyed.

The main impression from Africa's colourful and profuse social diversity is not confusion but the governing idea of unity. In a single sentence, Suzgo, a 20-year-old Ngoni from Zambia, revealed to me the essence of African societies. I had asked: 'How are you this morning, Suzgo?' The reply: 'I am very fine, since I came to your house and belonged.'

The feeling of belonging is vital to the individual in Africa, as it is for anybody anywhere. In Africa, the feeling is extrovert and manifest. The family, which always means the extended family, is the foundation of social life. Through kinship the family is interwoven in a network of obligation and reciprocity with the larger tribal society. The symbol of the clan totem, the facial scarification, the body decor and ornament, the uniform dress are less mysterious signs than they may appear. The sameness of the signs, literally and visibly, expresses that people are alike. I belong to you and you belong to me. Identity is achieved through social unity, not through individual achievement. Social security is achieved through the systematic development of family and kinship, not through a yearly instalment on a life insurance policy.

THE DOMINANCE OF THE TRANSNATIONAL EDUCATION INDUSTRY

Some of the major social changes taking place in Africa today can only be witnessed with sadness. Perhaps the real threat to a social transformation based on genuine sharing and equity for all is not foreign economic and technological dominance, but the dominance of the transnational education industry. Young people are uprooted from their culture, they labour in student factories through their most formative years in isolation from their own heritage, and they return reprocessed by the education industry as modernists with various professional labels. Intellectual credentials and skills are acquired; in the process, the ability to understand the old way of life is lost. The African standard is discarded in favour of a western modernist concept of social progress. Shame and scorn are expressed for the traditional way of life—the truest, the best and the only foundation for the social synthesis of the future Africa, a society which merges the good in the old and the best in the new.

Can such phenomena as cross-cultural communication and social transformation really be understood and directed? Perhaps, but only if you are really fond of people.

NOTES

1. Wittgenstein, Ludwig, *Philosophical Investigations*, Blackwells, Oxford, 1958.
2. Whorf, B. Lee, *Language, Thought and Reality*, MIT Press, Cambridge, Mass., 1974.
3. Cole, A., Gay, G., Click, J., Sharp, D., *The Cultural Context of Learning and Thinking*, Basic Books, New York, 1971.
4. Smythe, Dallas W., 'The Role of Mass Media and Popular Culture in Defining Development', Paper for the International Scientific Conference on Mass Communication and Social Consciousness in a Changing World, Leipzig, September 1974.
5. Bacchus, M.K., 'Structural Change and Transformation—Education and Development', Lead Paper, Commonwealth Conference on Non Formal Education for Development, New Delhi, January 1979.
6. Turnham, D., *Empirical Evidence of Open Unemployment in Developing Countries*, Third World Employment, Penguin Books, London, 1973.
7. Government of India, *Report of the Education Commission, 1964—66*, New Delhi, 1967.
8. Ashby, W. Ross, *An Introduction to Cybernetics*, Methuen & Co., London, 1976.
9. Smedslund, J., *Psykologi*, Universitetsforlaget, Oslo, 1967 (Norwegian).
10. Ibid.
11. Whorf, B. Lee, op. cit.
12. Wober, M., *Psychology in Africa*, International African Institute, London, 1975 and Mbiti, John S., *African religions and philosophy*, Heinemann, London, 1969.
13. Whorf, B. Lee, op. cit.
14. Stanner, W.E.H., 'The Dreaming', *Australian Signpost*, Sidney, 1956.
15. Whorf, B. Lee, op. cit.
16. Schmandt-Besserat, Denise, 'An Archaic Recording System and the Origin of Writing', *Syro-Mesopotamian Studies*, Vol. 1, Issue 2, Undena Publications, Basel, 1977.
17. Oppenheim, O. Leo, 'An Operational Device in Mesopotamian Bureaucracy', *Journal of Near Eastern Studies*, 17, 121—28, Chicago, 1958.
18. Amiet, Pierre, 'Il y a 5,000 ans les Elamites inventaient l'écriture', *Archéologia*, 12, 20—22, Paris, 1966.
19. Schmandt-Besserat, Denise, op. cit.
20. Ibid.
21. Ibid.
22. Piaget, J. and Inhelder, B., *La Psychologie de l'Enfant*, Presses Universitaires, Paris, 1967.
23. Fuglesang, A., *Applied Communication in Developing Countries*, Dag Hammarskjöld Foundation, Uppsala, 1973.
24. Whorf, B. Lee, op. cit.
25. Ibid.
26. Wittgenstein, Ludwig, op. cit.
27. Ibid.
28. Katz, D., *Gestaltpsychologie*, Benno Schwabe & Co., Basel, 1948.
29. Smedslund, J., op. cit.
30. Raum, O.I., *Chaga Childhood*, Oxford University Press, London, 1967.
31. Whorf, B. Lee, op. cit.
32. Egudu, R. and Nwoga, D., *Igbo Traditional Verse*, Heinemann, London, 1973.
33. Ibid.
34. Bateson, G., *Steps to an Ecology of Mind*, Paladin Books, London, 1978.

35. George, F.H., *Cybernetics*, Hodder & Stoughton, New York, 1971.

36. Cole, A., Gay, G., Click, J., Sharp, D., op. cit.

37. Farsi, S.S., *Swahili Sayings*, KLB, Nairobi, 1979.

38. Raum, O.I., op. cit.

39. Ibid.

40. Ibid.

41. Ibid.

42. Ocitti, J.P., *African Indigenous Education*, East African Literature Bureau, Kampala, 1973.

43. Raum, O.I., op. cit.

44. Middleton, John and Tait, David (eds), *Tribes Without Rulers: Studies in African Segmentary Systems*, London, 1958.

45. Ward, Colin, *Anarchy in Action*, George Allen & Unwin, London, 1973 and Ashby, W. Ross, *Cybernetics*, Methuen & Co., London, 1976.

46. Turnbull, Colin M., *The Forest People*, Pan Books, London, 1979.

Turnbull, Colin M., 'Some Observations Regarding the Experiences and Behaviour of the BaMbuti Pygmies', *American Journal of Psychology*, Austin, 1961.

47. Katz, D., op. cit.

48. Holmes, Alan C., *A Study of Understanding of Visual Symbols in Kenya*, Ovac, London, 1966.

Centre for Educational Development Overseas, *Visual Symbols Survey*, London, 1969.

49. Fuglesang, A., op. cit.

50. Fussel, D. and Haaland, A., *Communicating with Pictures in Nepal*, NDS/Unicef, Kathmandu, 1976.

51. Maclean, U., *Magical Medicine, a Nigerian Case Study*, Penguin Books, London, 1977.

52. Ibid.

53. Harley, G.W., *Native African Medicine*, F. Cass & Co., London, 1970.

54. Ibid.

55. Ibid.

56. Ibid.

57. Lewin, K., 'Forces Behind Food Habits and Methods of Change', *National Research Council Bulletin*, 108, Washington DC, 1943.

Yudkin, J. and McKenzie, I.C., *Changing Food Habits*, MacGibbon & Kee, London, 1964.

58. Church, M.A., 'Educational Methods, Cultural Characteristics and Nutrition Rehabilitation: Experience in Kampala Unit', *Environmental Child Health*, London, March 1971.

59. World Health Statistics, Vol. II, *Health Personnel and Hospital Establishments*, WHO, Geneva, 1979.

60. *North-South: A Programme for Survival*, The Report of the Independent Commission on International Development Issues under the Chairmanship of Willy Brandt, MIT Press, Cambridge, Mass., 1980 and Pan Books, London, 1980. See also The 1975 Dag Hammarskjöld Report, What Now: Another Development, *Development Dialogue* 1975: 1/2, Uppsala, 1975.

61. Sterky, G. and Molander, L. (eds), *Birth-Weight Distribution—An Indicator of Social Development*, SAREC Report No R-2, SAREC, Stockholm, 1978. See also *Development Dialogue* 1978:1, The Dag Hammarskjöld Foundation, Uppsala, 1978, especially pp 4-13.

62. Lee, R.B. and De Vere, I. (eds), *Kalahari Hunter-Gatherers, Studies of the !Kung San and their Neighbours*, Harvard University Press, Cambridge, Mass., 1976.